D1247195

Artists, Patrons, and the Public

ARTISTS, PATRONS, AND THE PUBLIC
Why Culture Changes

Barry Lord and Gail Dexter Lord

ALTAMIRA
PRESS

A division of
ROWMAN & LITTLEFIELD PUBLISHERS, INC.
Lanham • New York • Toronto • Plymouth, UK

Published by AltaMira Press
A division of Rowman & Littlefield Publishers, Inc.
A wholly owned subsidary of The Rowman & Littlefield Publishing Group, Inc.
4501 Forbes Boulevard, Suite 200, Lanham, Maryland 20706
http://www.altamirapress.com

Estover Road, Plymouth PL6 7PY, United Kingdom

British Library Cataloguing in Publication Information Available

Library of Congress Cataloging-in-Publication Data

Lord, Barry, 1939–
    Artists, patrons, and the public : why culture changes / Barry Lord and
Gail Dexter Lord.
        p. cm.
    ISBN 978-0-7591-1848-5 (cloth : alk. paper) —
    ISBN 978-0-7591-1901-7 (electronic)
    1. Arts and society. 2. Social change. I. Lord, Gail Dexter, 1946– II. Title. III.
Title: Why cultural changes.
    NX180.S6L67 2010
    701'.03—dc22   2009053108

Printed in the United States of America

✑ Contents

Illustrations

Acknowledgments

OUR thanks go first to the artists whom we have known, admired, or worked with over the years. They have inspired us, and their work continues to do so.

We must also extend our thanks to our clients, many of whom are either patrons themselves or are administrators of patronage institutions. Cultural institutions are sometimes in the vanguard, at other times merely in the grip of cultural change, and working with their managers and workers at all levels has taught us much of what we know about how cultural change affects not only the audiences of these institutions, but also those on their governing boards and staffs.

We are also grateful for the support of our own staff at Lord Cultural Resources. We have learned from all of them, past and present. For their work on the preparation of this book we thank particularly our former senior consultant Mira Goldfarb, who initially read and edited the text and found the images for the illustrations; Barbara Willis, Cecilia Faria, and Julie Kim, who secured the permissions for the illustrations; our production manager, Luca Vetere, who formatted the manuscript; Louis Choquette, who prepared the index; and as always, our executive assistant, Mira Ovanin.

Special thanks go to three very busy professionals in this field who took time to read and comment on an early version of our text: the distinguished historian of photography, Professor Marta Braun, director of photographic preservation and collections management in the School of Image Arts at Ryerson University in Toronto; the outstanding archaeologist of Meso-America, Dr. William Fash, director of the Peabody Museum at Harvard University; and the author of *Millennium, Truth: A History* and *Civilizations: Culture, Ambition and the Transformation of Nature*, among other books, Dr. Felipe Fernández-Armesto, a professorial fellow at Queen Mary College of the University of London and a member of the Modern History Faculty at

Oxford University. The book's shortcomings are entirely ours, but we thank all three for their very useful and apt comments, which helped us to avert some errors and omissions and at the same time gave us confidence that the book has an important message to deliver.

Even more important through her encouraging us to proceed with the book, giving it a first reading, and providing helpful hints to make it better was our daughter, Dr. Beth Lord, who is teaching philosophy at the University of Dundee in Scotland and took time to read our draft while working on her own books.

Finally, our thanks go to Jack Meinhardt of Rowman & Littlefield, the parent company of AltaMira Press, for committing his firm to the publication of a book that is clearly different from our Manuals series for museums that AltaMira had previously published. We also thank Marissa Parks of AltaMira and Julia Loy of Rowman & Littlefield for their editorial work in seeing the manuscript through to completion. We hope it is worthy of the commitment and contribution of all those who have worked on it with us.

Introduction

Why Does Culture Change?

"IF you gotta ask, you ain't never gonna know." So Louis Armstrong famously replied when he was asked what jazz is. It's a great answer because the key to understanding music and the arts is to experience them in an unqualified way.

But questions about culture persist and so does the hope for some answers. At a time when culture is changing at warp speed it seems worthwhile to ask ourselves: Why shouldn't culture remain the same? Could human culture achieve an ideal stage of development (as some Renaissance scholars thought it had in ancient Greece, and some Victorian scholars thought it had in the Renaissance) and just stay there, enriching and enhancing a stabilized set of values? Instead, both historically and today, the culture that surrounds us and the culture we live in are in constant flux—sometimes, it seems, capriciously.

For those who enroll in cultural studies or who read concert programs and the labels in art museums, cultural change is manifest in the sheer number of "isms" that seem to roll on and on: classicism, romanticism, realism, naturalism, mannerism, neoclassicism, pointillism, impressionism, futurism, cubism, expressionism, surrealism, modernism, postmodernism, and so on and on. The delight parents and young children experience in naming things seems to be writ large in the cultural realm—each change, each new idea, is named. But why does culture change? What are the forces of change?

Simple explanations abound—probably the most popular being "decade-ism," promoted mainly by nostalgia radio stations that feature the music of successive decades. This has matured into a mini-industry of exhibitions, documentaries, shows, and books purporting to explain the cultural changes of the 1920s, 1930s, 1950s, 1960s, or 1980s—reflected in lifestyles, architecture, fashion, film, music, or art—as arising from "history," understood as the mere passage of time organized by decade. While emotionally appealing, and providing an excellent marketing tool for fashion revivals, decade-ism is not much of an explanation if we are asking *why* culture changes. Recording the passage of trends is one thing; analyzing the process of cultural change is another.

"Generational change" provides another pop-psychology explanation for change: parents loved Frank Sinatra (1915–1998), but their children rebelled with Bob Dylan. While this approach has the virtue of expanding the decade to an approximate thirty-year generational time scale, it doesn't explain why there have been many cultures in which children revered and imitated the music of their elders for scores of generations over hundreds of years. Some cultural change is imperceptibly slow; some change is incredibly fast. Some change is subtle and hardly noticed, while other change is iconoclastic and destructive. Much Victorian architecture was torn down during the heyday of international modernism, but today it is modern buildings that are threatened. The culture and heritage of one group of people are often the targets of destructive campaigns by another during conflicts, civil wars, or throughout long-standing foreign occupation, domination, oppression, or "ethnic cleansing."

In the twenty-first century we have become even more keenly aware of cultural change due to issues of identity, migration, and globalization. Immigrant families the world over struggle with cultural change as their children more readily learn new languages, adopt new lifestyles, and witness alternative belief systems. On the one hand, we speak of "culture shock"; on the other, cultural diversity offers both old and new populations of many countries a generally richer range of alternatives than at any previous time in history. *Economic Development and Cultural Change* is the title of a scholarly journal addressing the ways in which these two topics relate to each other—or not—especially in developing countries.

It is not only people, groups, and nations that are seen to possess cultures, but also corporations, universities, hospitals, and many other institutions—most of them in need of cultural change, according to specialists in "change management."

The Canadian communications theorist Marshall McLuhan (1911–1980) is often associated with the argument that technology motivates cultural change, as articulated in his landmark books *The Mechanical Bride* and *The Gutenberg Galaxy*. However, his subsequent book *Understanding Media* is really about "understanding ourselves" because, as he explained, media are extensions of ourselves. Nowhere is his theory more prescient than with regard to today's cell phone technologies (which he did not live to see), which immeasurably extend human capacity to communicate in time and space. But are the technological advances of the Internet and Web 2.0 in themselves causes—or effects—of cultural change? However we perceive it, digital communication is clearly a primary phenomenon in cultural change today and conditions much of what we have written in this book; but it is not in itself an explanation.

The intensity of cultural change in our own time has made understanding it a matter of urgent interest. This book asks the question "Why?" and proposes some answers. Our approach focuses on aesthetic culture and is mainly practical in orientation, based on the lifetime of cultural practice of the authors. In this introduction it may be useful for the reader to learn a little of what that practice has been about.

Barry Lord began as an apprentice actor at the Shakespearian Festival Theatre in Stratford, Canada, and was a published poet as well as a student of philosophy, first at McMaster University in Hamilton, Canada, then, focusing on the history and philosophy of religion, at the Center for the Study of World Religions at Harvard. Gail Dexter Lord, a history graduate from the University of Toronto, began her career by organizing a pop culture festival at that institution and as an art critic for Canada's largest-circulation newspaper, the *Toronto Star*, and then as a lecturer in art history at what is now the School of Image Arts at Ryerson University in Toronto. Meanwhile Barry, who has also written art criticism, edited Canada's national art magazine, *artscanada* (1967), and authored books of art history, including his 1973 *History of Painting in Canada: Toward a People's Art*, had begun a lifetime of work in museums and galleries, including education and curatorial roles in the 1960s and '70s with the National Gallery of Canada in Ottawa, the Vancouver Art Gallery, the New Brunswick Museum in Saint John, and at Expo '67 in Montreal. Barry has also taught creative writing at a college in Kitchener and art history in both English and French at universities in Guelph, Montreal, Ottawa, and Toronto.

In 1981 we founded Lord Cultural Resources, a company that has grown to become the world's largest firm specializing in the planning and management of cultural institutions. Having engaged in almost 2,000 cultural projects in around forty-five countries on six continents, we have lived and worked in environments where cultural change is being created. Along with our colleagues in the company (known in Spain as *Lordcultura*, elsewhere in Europe as *Lordculture*, and as *SinoLord* in China), we are deeply involved in providing planning and management services related to changes in physical facilities, tangible and non-tangible heritage, exhibitions, performances, altered governance structures, and long-range strategic planning for communities and institutions of all kinds. The diversity of our clients in geography, in subject focus, and in goals has continuously challenged any fixed ideas about culture we might have harbored and led us to what we believe is a dynamic vision of cultural change. Two years after founding the company, we set down a first draft of the analysis and principles in this book—and we have ever since been refining and adjusting them to accord with our practical experience around the world.

Our earliest Canadian clients were small communities—from Acadian settlements in Prince Edward Island to pulp and paper towns in British Columbia—struggling to find a voice and establish cultural institutions on a professional basis. At the time of this writing, we are engaged in an equally compelling struggle to help establish Canada's newest national museum in Winnipeg (the first outside Ottawa), the Canadian Museum for Human Rights. The new CMHR caps three or four decades of cultural change that we have witnessed across our country.

In the United States, where we have conducted numerous assignments for art museums including the Art Institute of Chicago, the Los Angeles County Museum of Art, and the Brooklyn Museum of Art, we learned first hand about the decisive role of cultural patrons and were inspired by the possibilities of cultural institutions anchored in civil society. Recently we were privileged to have assisted the new National Museum of African American History and Culture come to life on the Smithsonian Mall in Washington at the very time that the United States was inaugurating its first African-American president. That is cultural change writ large!

The intensity with which cities that had become derelict as a result of deindustrialization fought first for revitalization and then for leadership in the knowledge economy has taught us a lot about cultural change. Curating the *Glasgow's Glasgow* exhibition in that city's year as European City of Culture (1990); planning The Lowry in Salford, England; programming the Louvre's new branch at Lens in northern France; and developing a strategic plan for the Museo Guggenheim in Bilbao, Spain, were transformative experiences in cultural change.

In Johannesburg, we saw how social and political struggle leads to cultural change when, working with inspired teams of South African artists, historians, preservationists, and urban planners, we helped to transform a place of colonial oppression, the Old Fort prison, into a place called Constitution Hill that celebrates the most liberal constitution in the world, while preserving and interpreting the infamous prison that at different times held both Mahatma Gandhi (1869–1948) and Nelson Mandela. Physically integrated with South Africa's new Constitutional Court, the exhibition and programming at Constitution Hill communicates not only the horrors of the site's former uses, but also the way in which that suffering and the fight to end it led to the hope expressed in the new, powerfully democratic Constitutional Court building and the cultural precinct that surrounds it.

New art museums that we have recently helped to plan in Poland, Estonia, Latvia, Russia, and Turkey provide living examples of how closely connected are political and cultural change. Our current work with leaders in the United Arab Emirates, Bahrain, and Saudi Arabia demonstrates what the desire for cultural change can accomplish toward creating openness and intercultural understanding. Our Asian clients have impressed on us a fact that we might in theory have found hard to believe: non-Western societies can embrace Western cultural forms once seen as vestiges of colonialism, and now that they are fully independent, these countries can infuse these Western institutions, media, formats, or styles with their own cultural meanings. We have experienced this transformation while working with a new city museum in Jaipur, India; in Singapore, where we helped develop a heritage museum system that the island republic is making a place of discourse on citizenship in that city-state; in Bangkok, where our clients conceived the Thai Creative and Design Center; in programming the new National Museum of Korea in Seoul; and in many projects in China, from the planning, design, and management of the construction and installation of the Hong Kong Heritage Museum to programming the expansion of the National Art Museum of China in Beijing. In 2008 our work with museums around the world was the subject of a one-hour television documentary called *Museum Maestros,* shown on the Bravo! TV network.

World's fairs are both a medium of cultural change and a measure of it. We have had the opportunity to participate in the representation of cultural change in world's fairs beginning with Barry's curation of the *Paintings in Canada* exhibition for Expo '67 in Montreal and continuing through planning the Canadian pavilions at Expo '92 in Seville (Spain) and Expo '93 in Taejon (Korea) to managing development of the theme pavilions at Expo

2000 in Hannover (Germany) and planning post-Expo use of the site for Expo 2008 in Zaragoza, Spain.

While attending to our practical work worldwide, we have also been teaching and contributing to the growing literature on cultural change in the museum field. *Planning Our Museums* was our first book of this kind, published in 1983 by the National Museums of Canada (also published in French as *La Planification de Musées*). To our surprise, we discovered that it was also the world's first book on the subject, and that it was put into use by museum professionals and in museum studies courses from Rome to Sydney.

In 1988, together with John Nicks (then a principal in our company), we undertook a study of the costs of collection management and care in Britain's museums for the UK government agency then responsible for museums and libraries. Our report on this very practical question of cultural change—the cost of the documentation, preservation, and management of artifacts, specimens, and works of art—was greeted as the first and only systematic study of this subject and was published in the following year by Her Majesty's Stationery Office (HMSO) as a book entitled *The Cost of Collecting*.

HMSO was so impressed with the interest shown in that volume that we were asked to develop *The Manual of Museum Planning*, which became a classic of museum literature after it first appeared in 1991. The series, now published in the United States by AltaMira Press, continued with *The Manual of Museum Management* (1997), *The Manual of Museum Exhibitions* (2002), *The Manual of Museum Learning* (2007), and *The Manual of Strategic Planning for Museums* (coauthored by Gail Lord and Kate Markert, 2007). Reflecting the incessant pace of cultural change, the series has required periodic updates. A second edition of *The Manual of Museum Planning* appeared in 1999, and a second of *The Manual of Museum Management* followed in 2009. By that time the latter text had already been translated into Spanish, Russian, Chinese, and Georgian. Cultural workers in Georgia have been particularly engaged with using the Manuals as a guide to their work, having translated also the large *Manual of Museum Exhibitions* and using the books in their training programs and as handbooks in their daily practice.

As their titles suggest, the Manual series has been intensely practical. This book on cultural change draws on all our experience to respond to more fundamental questions: Why does culture change? What is culture? How is it generated—by individuals or by groups of people in relation to one another? What is the role of patronage in the arts? And how do we understand the role of the artist? We believe that a dynamic theory of culture emerges from this inquiry that can serve as the basis for a more effective way not only of understanding culture, but also of participating creatively in the process of cultural change.

This book thus offers an approach to understanding the roots of culture based on the experiences of two lifetimes of immersion in cultural work. From our early years as cultural critics and political activists to today we have often found ourselves trying to explain why culture matters to those for whom culture is marginal. Those early debates mark the beginning of the thinking that led by a thousand journeys to this book.

The book proposes a vocabulary for thinking and talking and writing about culture that is intended to be integrative, multidisciplinary, and interdisciplinary. In doing so, we are using terminology in ways that may not satisfy any one of the disciplines we hope to bring together—archaeology, anthropology, art history, social history, and cultural studies among them. Practitioners in each of these disciplines are likely to find that our analysis and terminology differ from the current usage in their individual fields, but our practice has enabled—and required—us to develop a syncretistic understanding of cultural change.

Artists, Patrons, and the Public is intended for artists; for students and teachers of art history, museum studies, and philosophy; and for cultural workers in all media and disciplines. But it is also intended for all those who may think of themselves first as members of the audience for the arts, because in fact we are *all* participating constantly in cultural change. Our hope is that by becoming more conscious of the principles governing these changes everyone may contribute to achieving and enjoying a future in the twenty-first century that realizes more of the vast potential of global diversity that is now available to us in ways that it never was before.

CHAPTER 1

What Is Culture?

FOR some people, culture is something alien and not to be trusted; for others, it is a deeply held conviction about their way of life that they believe is misunderstood or undervalued by outside authorities who rank and judge culture; for still others, the acquisition of culture is a mark of social distinction and the ability to keep up with cultural change—the greatest distinction of all. All of these are examples of not feeling comfortable in one's own cultural skin.

Discomfort with one's own culture was evident in the council chambers of the city of Salford in England in 1996 when the council was about to vote on building a new cultural center. A suburb of Manchester, Salford was made famous in *The Condition of the Working Class in England in 1844* by Friedrich Engels (1820–1895) as one of the most horrific examples in the world of the immiseration of working people as a result of the industrial revolution. Salford, 150 years later, was much improved, but the world had also moved on, and according to European Union statistics, the city was at the center of the most deprived area of Europe in the mid-1990s. So Salford's left-leaning council was in the process of implementing an amazing forty-year vision: to transform the filthy, stinking Manchester ship canal, which had become disused in the 1950s, into a twenty-first-century leisure waterway at the heart of a new Salford, replete with hotels, condominiums, shopping, high-tech industries, and cultural facilities.

The canal had been rebuilt and the water cleaned, so a cultural center was the next item on the agenda. The first idea had been to build an iconic opera house (as in Sydney, Australia), but this proposal never gained traction with the local population. Now a new consultant team, including ourselves, was recommending a cultural center featuring more accessible theaters and a new home for Salford's major collection of paintings and drawings by L. S. Lowry (1887–1976). Lowry is the most popular artist in England—so popular there is a song school children learn about "matchstick men" after the way that Lowry portrayed the working classes of Salford and Manchester going to and from the factories, fighting, drinking, and enjoying fairs and the seaside. Lowry, who earned his living as a rent collector in the poorest districts of the region, was the consummate artist depicting the character of working-class life and people. His paintings are occasionally purchased at auction by successful British rock musicians of working-class background, but are little-known internationally and are infrequently on display in major art galleries. In the 1990s, the Tate for example owned eight works by Lowry, but at its London location (now called Tate Britain) Lowry was one of the artists most requested by the public, because his works were rarely on view.

L. S. Lowry (1887–1976), *Coming from the Mill*, 1930, oil on canvas, 42 x 52 cm (16 ½ x 20½ in.), The Lowry Collection, Salford, England. Photo: © The Lowry Collection, Salford.

Having listened to our presentation, and having noted the not inconsiderable costs of the project, the leader of the council looked searchingly at Gail and asked, "But is Lowry any good? How can you be sure?"

The answer was a long one, and is the subject of this chapter. It was persuasive enough to get the go-ahead from council. The Lowry, as the cultural center was named, opened in 2000, its architects, Michael Wilford & Partners, winning an award for the best cultural building of the millennium year. Its success attracted the Imperial War Museum North to locate next door; a Lowry shopping center was soon thriving nearby, and today The Lowry is the center of a vibrant reborn Salford with more than $3 billion of inward investment and 6,500 new jobs. Salford's transformation is so complete that the city won the competition for location of the British Broadcasting Corporation's northern production facilities.

The Lowry story in the Salford context is a particularly interesting example of how to understand what culture is and why it matters: a popular artist, who represents a way of life, serious enough to be in major public

Michael Wilford, architect, *The Lowry*, 2000, Salford, England. Photo: Len Grant.

collections, but not serious enough to be known internationally nor to be the subject of extensive study by major curators. Whether he is a good artist or not is essentially an aesthetic judgment: I explained to the council how aesthetic judgments are formed, that there are different schools of aesthetics and that these change over time. I told them what a number of curators had written about as being significant in Lowry's work—particularly the way he expressed alienation, a major subject of modern art. But the most powerful argument was that Lowry's works have a uniquely important meaning when displayed in Salford because that is where they were created: Salford provides the context for *why* they were created. In that sense, whether Tate shows Lowry or not is not nearly as significant as the public dialogue that the people of Salford and their visitors can have with these works that are so much part of the local culture.

What do we mean by the "culture" of Salford? We need to begin with a definition. Unfortunately, definitions of "culture" are legion, and varied. As the English social critic Raymond Williams (1921–1988) observed in his 1976 book *Keywords: A Vocabulary of Culture and Society* (Fontana Press, London), "culture" is "one of the two or three most complicated words in the English language."

Changes in the meaning of the word over time are themselves indicative of the roots of cultural change: derived from the past participle of the Latin verb *colare*, meaning "to tend to," "care for," or "preserve," the medieval usage of *cultura* and its variants in western European languages referred to cultivation of the land, at the time when that was the chief source of wealth. During the Renaissance, in the late fifteenth and early sixteenth century, when intellectual pursuits took on a new importance in all aspects of society—including the economy—the word began to be used as a metaphor to refer to cultivation of the mind. This originally metaphorical meaning was gradually extended in the encyclopedic eighteenth century and the romantic early nineteenth century to connote the mental, spiritual, and aesthetic characteristics of groups of people. By 1869 Matthew Arnold (1822–1888), in his book *Culture and Anarchy*, was using the word in a broader context, to refer to civilization as a whole. The term "civilization" has its own unhappy history as a mark of distinction between highly elaborated cultures of (usually) imperial powers and the supposedly simpler cultures of the colonized.

Throughout the twentieth century many writers have observed the deficiencies in Arnold's Victorian approach, which disdains any serious consideration of mass culture or popular culture. In 1958, Williams countered Arnold's "high culture" with his own "ordinary culture"—which would not have been much help for Salford's councilors, who precisely needed to know that their big investment in Lowry was not for something merely "ordinary." Still today there are repeated undertakings to define "popular culture," "mass culture," and "people's culture," as distinguished from "high culture," "fine art," or "civilization," multiplying the range of possible combinations and unfortunately often compounding confusion as they go.

Still more unfortunate have been attempts to define "art" without first defining "culture." Leo Tolstoy (1828–1910) asked "What is art?" in the title of his essay on the subject, and many philosophers, critics, and art historians have attempted answers, assuming that this is the most profound and basic question. In 1914, the art critic Clive Bell (1881–1964) insisted that art is "significant form." Others have countered with theories of art as individual expression or as a critical response to social realities, or have suggested that art is the result of activities that are essentially non-productive in the sense of economic growth. Whatever one may think of these theories, it is noteworthy that in one way or another each assigns a *passive* role to art—a passivity that is completely contrary to our experience of art that is powerful, transformative, and meaningful—sometimes shockingly so. We need to define art in a way that acknowledges its dynamic role in our personal experience, and in the world—which is to say that we need to define art in relation to culture as a whole.

All attempts to define art, whether formalist, expressionist, or socially relevant, will fail if they do not situate art within a general theory of culture.

That was the lesson we took from Salford—the aesthetic judgement of L. S. Lowry will change over time; his relevance to the culture of the region is an indelible fact that will endure. And although their relevance to their own cultures may not always be as immediately obvious, the same is true of all artists.

The rise of anthropology as a scientific discipline in the late nineteenth and through the twentieth century has come to the rescue by extending the definition of culture to include all aspects of human activity related to our social existence, which is the meaning we know today. So much so that by the mid-twentieth century, American anthropologists Alfred Kroeber (1876–1960) and Clyde Kluckhohn (1905–1960) were able to cite no fewer than 164 definitions of culture in their book *Culture: A Critical Review of Concepts and Definitions* (reprinted in 1978). Kroeber and Kluckhohn grouped the definitions in eight categories:

- Topical definitions, in which culture consists of everything on a list of topics such as social organization, religion, and economy
- Historical definitions, for which culture is received social heritage, passed on to future generations in turn
- Behavioral definitions, stressing the learned character of culture
- Normative definitions, emphasizing the ideals or values that culture prescribes
- Functional definitions, for which culture is the way human beings adapt to the environment and to each other
- Mental or cerebral definitions, seeing culture as a complex of ideas and learned habits
- Structural definitions, emphasizing the ways in which ideas, symbols, and behaviors are interrelated
- Symbolic definitions, focused on the meanings shared by a society

Understood in this way, culture is an enormous subject: the anthropological *Outline of Cultural Materials* (*OCM*), first developed by George Murdock (1897–1985) and others for a cross-cultural survey at Yale University in 1937, listed 79 major divisions and 637 subdivisions of cultural activities. Hunting, fishing, and gathering, for instance, were seen as subdivisions of the division devoted to seeking food. (Still in use today, the *OCM* is now available online.)

This vast range indicates that any definition of culture should begin with an understanding that culture is *active*. It is not a reflex, a reflection or product of some other activity. It is not a product of our socialization, it is the very act or process of becoming socialized. It is a dynamic part of our experience and of the world. It is a transformative activity in itself. The very identity of individuals who participate in cultural change—as we all do—is itself continually being formed, reformed, and transformed by their cultural agency.

Culture does not appear to be a *uniquely* human activity. Recent research is persuasive in suggesting that there are other animal species in our world that may also be considered "cultural species." Contemporary philosophers remind us of the need to transcend anthropocentrism and to see all human activity as part of nature. There may well be interesting comparisons to be made among the various cultural species. However, this book is focused on understanding human culture, and more specifically human aesthetic culture—a big enough job.

While culture may not be uniquely human, our definition of culture as an active force in the world must acknowledge that it is clearly a *fundamental* aspect of all human activity. Culture is not only pervasive, it underlies everything we think, say, and do. Beyond a few basic instincts, human infants depend on learning to grow up, and what they are learning as they grow up is culture. This is not to deny but rather to affirm the importance of nature as well as nurture. Matt Ridley's 2003 book, *Nature via Nurture: Genes, Experience, and What Makes Us Human,*[1] reviews the past century of literature on this contentious topic, bringing it up to date with the current understanding of the genome, and summarizes the convincing case made by specialists in many disciplines for the interpenetration of nature and nurture in the growth of an individual and in the evolution of human society as a whole.

If we understand nurture as the process of learning our culture, but we also appreciate that nurture is rooted in nature, we may then see how thoroughly culture is imbedded in nature, while at the same time being distinguishable from it as a transforming agent, a catalyst within the natural environment. The relationship between culture and nature may therefore be best described as the *transformation* of nature into culture, but only if we understand that the transformation effected by culture is itself rooted in nature, so that the culture that results is wholly integrated with the natural environment that is being transformed. Historian Felipe Fernández-Armesto explores this relationship extensively in his *Civilizations: Culture, Ambition, and the Transformation of Nature,*[2] where he classifies civilizations in relation to the environments from which they spring, yet insists that a society is "civilized in direct proportion to its distance, its difference from the unmodified natural environment."

So culture is about our transformation of nature. But it is also about our societies. At Salford we learned that culture is about us. Culture is about human relationships. The human cultural agent cannot learn culture and cannot behave culturally alone, but must always act and react in relation to others, either an actually present respondent or an imagined future audience. *Culture is inherently social.* Thus culture must involve the transformation of society as well as nature. In observing this transformative character of culture in relation to society, we do not mean to suggest any nineteenth-century notion of social "progress," nor to imply any "natural law" of constant social change. Maintaining cultural or social stasis—or trying to—may itself be the very act of transformation of society that is needed by at least some agents in certain times and places. Sustaining a culture requires a constant process of social transformation just as much as making changes in it.

With this awareness that both culture and human society are as much embedded in nature as they are distinct from it, we arrive at a definition of culture that is both active and broad, dynamic and—mercifully—brief:

Culture is the transformation of nature and society that is fundamental to all human activity.

NOTES

1. Matt Ridley, *Nature via Nurture: Genes, Experience, and What Makes Us Human* (New York: HarperCollins, 2003).

2. Felipe Fernández-Armesto, *Civilizations: Culture, Ambition, and the Transformation of Nature* (New York: Free Press, 2001).

CHAPTER 2

Four Kinds of Culture

PEOPLE say we work "in the cultural field," meaning the arts. Yet as we have just defined it, culture is a much broader activity than only the arts. Culture is the transformation of nature and society that is fundamental to all human activity. This anthropological definition means that culture has a vast range, so that we now need to differentiate between the major kinds or types of culture. Through our numerous assignments with diverse people in many regions of the world, we have come to understand four kinds of culture, for which we use the following four terms: material culture, physical culture, social/political culture, and aesthetic culture—the latter being the main focus of this book on cultural change.

Material culture is best understood as the transformation of the material environment around us that is necessary for survival.[1] Food and drink, shelter from the elements, and clothing where we need it for warmth are all material necessities appropriated by humans from nature.

For hundreds of millennia, Paleolithic hunters, fishers, and gatherers exploited the flora and fauna, the topography and climate around them. In the Neolithic period, pastoralists began herding animals, another way of transforming nature. The new methods of food production that Australian-born anthropologist Vere Gordon Childe (1892–1957) called the "Neolithic Revolution" (which were gradually introduced in many regions over thousands of years) marked a far more radical change in the way we transform the soils and plants around us to raise our food. Today, not only farmers but also workers in dairies, textile mills, and on housing projects are among the millions who continue to extend our material culture, transforming nature into the products of human manufacture for basic human needs.

With the greater complexity of contemporary society those needs have multiplied—transportation, for instance, has become basic to the survival of people who live at some distance from where they do the work that earns their food, shelter, and clothing. As noted in chapter 8, a source of energy is a basic need for all societies. And our understanding of material reality has deepened—physics, chemistry, and biology are among the sciences that contribute to our material culture today. Technologies based on these physical and life sciences have become dominant parts of our material culture. Material culture today comprises all mining and most manufacturing, excepting only the manufacture of goods, facilities, or equipment for the other three types of culture. It also extends to all the sciences and technologies needed for material culture production.

Physical culture includes all the activities needed to maintain our bodies in health, not only to prolong our own lives but also to make it possible for us to procreate, in order that the next generation may take our place. When material culture is at a minimum subsistence level, there is little physical culture and life expectancy is extremely low. The risk of the mother's death in childbirth has been very high throughout most of human existence. Yet birth and the survival of babies is essential to our survival as a species. Physical culture may have been begun by women caring for and advising their daughters, sisters, or granddaughters before conception, during pregnancy, and in childbirth and after. Health sciences, medicine, psychology, sports, hair salons, courtship, seduction and marriage customs, early childhood education, childcare, and fitness clubs are all part of physical culture today. Physical culture has been so successful that the sheer numbers of *Homo sapiens* and our lengthening life spans have allowed us to dominate the planet.

Material and physical culture may be considered *basic* because they are necessary to the perpetuation of human life on earth. Without material culture the individual would perish for want of food, shelter, or protection from the elements. Without physical culture not only would our own bodies wither, but we would also lose the capacity to reproduce our species. Material culture is among humans part of what Charles Darwin called "natural selection," while physical culture is for our species an aspect of what he called "sexual selection." These two basic types of culture are thus closely related to the evolution of the human species.

Hypothetically, we could conceive of a human society in which only these two basic types of culture were available. Sustained by a subsistence economy, it would appear to be at least possible that "man might live by bread alone." Yet even in societies where the struggle for existence in a challenging environment would appear to be all-consuming—such as among the traditional Inuit peoples of the high Arctic—we find that they developed a highly imaginative world of song, dance, story telling, and visualization. In circumpolar countries like Canada where some contemporary Inuit are only two generations away from living in a subsistence economy, elders can tell us much about their ways of life and culture when they lived entirely on the land. There were times of famine, but there were also times of plenty— times we could describe in economic terms as times of *surplus*.

The ability of material and physical culture not only to supply our needs but also to produce a surplus is what makes the other two types of culture both *possible* and *necessary*. After a successful hunt, there will be—at least temporarily—more food than the hunters can eat right away, so the question arises of what to do with that surplus, and how to distribute it. If there is a method of keeping it, then the questions become more complex—how and where will it be stored, and who will have access to it? These are questions of social organization, which we classify as the third kind of culture, *social-political culture*.

In light of the limited potential for hunting, fishing, and gathering wild foods today, we may think that such surplus was then rare. In fact, during the period of hunting and gathering, game, fish, and wild food plants were far more plentiful in many parts of the world. As late as the mid-nineteenth century there are common reports of the sky being darkened by the wings of passenger pigeons flying overhead—a species soon thereafter made extinct by human predation. Elders among the Crees in northern Quebec recall the far more plentiful geese that used to fly overhead for hunting only a few generations ago.

The indigenous Northwest Coast nations of Canada provide an outstanding example of a culture of surplus, where a few weeks' work when the salmon were running enabled each village to catch and then smoke and store food for the rest of the year. The civilization that resulted is one in which giving away surplus in the potlatch ceremony—in the form of cultural artifacts such as woven blankets or coppers, thereby demonstrating the donor's status—was a spectacular resolution to the question of how to control access to the surplus.[2]

With the advent of pastoralism and especially with more sedentary modes of agriculture in many parts of the world, the formerly intermittent questions of how to control access to stored surplus material culture became permanent, abiding issues. Granary doors and the keys to them were impor-

Controlling access to surplus grain: Unknown artist, Mali, door of a granary with images of ancestors, wood, and iron, 100 x 52 cm (39¼ x 20½ in.), Castello Sforzesco, Milan. Photo: Scala/Art Resource, NY.

tant cultural artifacts for many traditional West African agricultural nations. So were the stools on which rulers in some societies originally sat to guard access to the grain—a job subsequently delegated to armed men, as the stools sometimes evolved into thrones.

Surplus is a relative term. In a desert environment, or even on high dry plains, potable water may be so scarce that access to even a limited source may constitute control of a vital surplus. Regulating who gets or maintains access to that source becomes a vital question for the social-political and material culture of the people living in that environment. The same may be said of access to sources of surplus energy—a subject we return to in chapter 8.

Questions of how to distribute surplus material culture affect physical culture as well. Does the successful hunter or his family eat before others? Should shamans be given special privileges if they can cure the sick? What is the status of midwives who can save the lives of women giving birth? What is to be done with those who take some of the material surplus even though they are not considered to have the right to do so? Should surplus water or other vital resources be shared with strangers, as well as guests?

Physical culture can also create surplus—a surplus of time, as lives are prolonged sufficiently to allow more leisure, and a surplus of lives, as families grow larger and generations live longer. Like material surplus, such a surplus of time arises even in the earliest hunter-gatherer societies; indeed, many hunter-gatherer groups had and have more leisure time than agricultural or industrial ones. In all societies, combining the surplus of time produced by physical culture with the surplus of food, clothing, and shelter produced by material culture—stone for building, wood for carving, plants for weaving—makes *aesthetic culture*, the fourth kind of culture, possible.

Consider the carving of a polar bear in ivory by an artist of the Old Dorset or Thule Inuit culture. Its tiny proportions testify to the extremely limited material surplus of this high Arctic culture, as well as to the need for a carving so small that it can be held in the hand or sewn into the lining of a parka and carried long distances as a talisman by itinerant hunters and their families. Its subject matter, too, is close to the life of the hunt. Yet even in this near-subsistence culture, a little material surplus and the extra time afforded by success of the hunt—or necessitated by the wish to make the next hunt more successful—has resulted in a minute but magnificent work of sculpture.

Another way to show the connection between the two basic types of culture and aesthetic culture is to observe that surplus produced by material

Major sculpture with minimal resources: Unknown Dorset or Thule artist, Central Arctic, Canada, 11th–17th c., ivory, 1.4 x 0.8 x 3.3 cm (½ x ¼ x 1¼ in.), McCord Museum, Montreal, gift of Arctic Institute of North America (M21060). Photo: © McCord Museum.

and physical culture is universally manifested by the development of specialized roles for different members of a society. Within a social group with sufficient surplus there will be enough time and people not only for the controlling roles of those who guard access to the surplus, but potentially also for specialized occupations, such as weavers, carvers, musicians, or potters. The products of these specialized workers may be material culture artifacts, but they may also be instances of aesthetic culture—works of art or craft. Not all societies will have or need the complete range of specialized skills, but as the Inuit example illustrates, in all cases at least a minimum of surplus time and material is needed to support any of them. It's important to keep this fundamental truth in view despite the many examples of aesthetic culture arising in conditions of comparative privation—for all require some surplus of time or material.

Aesthetic culture consists of the meanings created in objects or by actions that are made possible and in some cases necessary by the surplus resulting from material and physical culture. It is most important that these meanings are apprehended, understood, and appreciated by our senses, and/or by our imagination, which is an extension of our senses. Although understanding the work of James Joyce (1882–1941) or Arnold Schoenberg (1874–1951) may be mentally taxing, the meaning intended by either artist must ultimately be apprehended by our senses, often amplified by our imagination. Aesthetic culture historically and today—the whole range of visual and performing arts, cultural heritage, and cultural industries—is the subject of the next chapter and the focus of the rest of this book.

Before passing on to consider aesthetic culture more closely, we need to distinguish it from and relate it to the third type, social-political culture. As we have already noted, resolving the issues of who controls the surplus generated by material and physical culture, and maintaining that resolution in practice, requires this third type of culture. Like aesthetic culture, social-political culture is made both *possible* and *necessary* by the surplus generated by material and physical culture, but social-political culture differs from aesthetic culture in that it must be apprehended, understood, and agreed to intellectually, rather than sensually, in order to be effective.

Especially when there is sufficient surplus to store, even for a season, social organization is needed to determine who will gain access to the stored grain or other foodstuffs, so political structures must become longer lasting. People need to believe in these structures if they are to be accepted, so they must be given meanings, and belief in those meanings must be enforced. When the shift to agriculture is pervasive, and especially if it involves a monoculture, as it did in the Nile valley, for instance, these structures must become permanent and unquestioned as the only viable way of life for the entire society, with religious beliefs invoked to reinforce these controls.

Thus, like aesthetic culture, social-political culture also comprises meanings—the meanings of social class distinctions, control of access to property, and the way the family, the clan, the tribe, or the village are organized. Social-political culture became far more advanced after the advent of agriculture, especially along those river valleys where monocultures began to be planted and harvested, creating great surplus storage of food and the need to control access to it. The meanings of the social distinctions in these societies—ancient Egypt, Mesopotamia, and China, especially—had to be clearly communicated and rigorously enforced. Politics and economics remain central to this type of culture today, explaining the meanings inherent in capitalist, socialist, or other relationships that determine access to the surplus our global society is capable of producing. Advertising has become strategically important to the distribution of surplus goods just as public relations helps regulate relations of power and powerlessness. These are part of social-political culture as are the academic disciplines of sociology, history, and philosophy.

Although aesthetic and social-political culture are both engendered by the surplus resulting from material and physical culture, the key distinction between them is that the meanings of aesthetic culture are apprehended, understood, and appreciated primarily by our *senses* and our imagination, which extends our senses, whereas the meanings of social-political culture are primarily understood cognitively or *intellectually*. Of course there is conceptual and intellectual content to all aesthetic culture (as the very term "concept art" reminds us), and there is a sensual content to much social and political culture. Both types of culture may be imbued and transmitted with emotion. Yet the distinction holds—we appreciate aesthetic culture primarily through our senses, whereas we learn social-political culture primarily through cognition. In philosophical terms, these means of apprehension, comprehension, and interpretation of our world and its history are sometimes referred to as *hermeneutics*. Thus there is a hermeneutic differentiation between aesthetic culture and social-political culture.

Seen from this standpoint, religion is an interesting cross-cultural phenomenon. Because it claims to determine the ultimate meanings of things and behavior—of life itself—religion is part of social-political culture. Yet many of its means of expression and communication of these meanings are aesthetic in character, combining sensual apprehension with intellectual meanings. Drawing its power from both the social-political and aesthetic realms accounts for the continuing hold of religion on generations of people.

As we said in the previous chapter, culture is *active*, not a passive reflection of other domains of experience. Both aesthetic culture and social-political culture are more than mere reflections of material and physical culture. While enabled by the surplus means and surplus time created by material and physical culture, both in turn have a strong influence on material and physical culture. Political organization, for example, directly affects the way people are organized to produce material culture, while religious beliefs directly alter physical culture by teaching and controlling social relations vital to reproduction, such as restrictions on the role of women. Although it may take longer to achieve its effects, aesthetic culture also actively influences all other types of culture: as English poet Percy Bysshe Shelley (1792–1822) wrote in *A Defence of Poetry* in 1821, "poets are the unacknowledged legislators of mankind."

Societies that have produced great surpluses in material culture and significant surpluses of time through excelling in physical culture often evolve highly elaborate social or political systems and an aesthetic culture replete with what are called "masterpieces." For much of the nineteenth and twentieth centuries, societies that lacked such surpluses owing to geography, resources, or social/political control by outsiders who appropriated those surpluses of material wealth (for example, cotton) or physical wealth (for example, through slavery) were often considered to be culturally "primitive." In the twenty-first century, globalization of information, education, and the increasing wealth of the world as a whole have stimulated a sense of identity and a desire to live within one's own culture in many of these societies. Nonetheless, many people in rapidly developing countries have a difficult time seeing value in their own aesthetic culture.

In the Philippines, for example, where we helped to develop a new gallery for the National Museum in 1997, even some of the museum's supporters and funders told us "Our ancient culture is not important; we didn't have many gold objects or great ceramics like other ancient civilizations." Working with the museum curators, we learned that the cultural wealth of the early Philippines was in its people and their intangible heritage—their stories, music, languages, and the extraordinary navigation abilities that allowed them to trade among the more than 10,000 islands of what is now their country. And so the new National Museum gallery was named *The Story of the Filipino People.* Sadly, the economic and political culture of the Philippines has significantly held back its material cultural development, so that in the early twenty-first century the country's greatest export is still its people, in the form of remittance workers who make the world a better place by their abilities to build, to teach, to clean, and to care for others, sending home a significant part of their earnings to their families left behind.

This chapter indicates not only that there are four kinds of culture, but also that there is an active interrelation among these four types of culture, each continually affecting and being influenced by the other three. This is a theme that we will return to again and again in this book. In the next chapter, however, we consider aesthetic culture more closely, defining our terms and making distinctions so that we can make sense when we talk about art.

NOTES

1. We are not limiting the use of the term "material culture" to material objects, as is often done in anthropological or archaeological discourse.

2. We insist on using the term "civilization" for all societies, not just for those that are literate, urban, or socially complex, as was the prejudicial practice in the past.

CHAPTER 3

The Meanings of Art

THE earliest forms of aesthetic culture that have been found to date may be the strands of shells in ancient graves in Africa and elsewhere. Traces of ochre in graves in what is now southern France are other early examples, again associated with mourning for the dead. Other important early media, not as evident to archeologists, are body painting and immaterial aesthetic culture like song and dance. These manifestations almost certainly predate the famous cave paintings of southern France and the celebrated stone carvings of mostly female figures, such as the so-called Venus of Willendorf; the earliest flutes have been found on gravesites in Germany. As a design sensibility was applied to utilitarian objects, basket weaving, clothing, and ceramics broadened the range of aesthetic culture still further.

The meanings intended by many of these early examples are not always immediately apparent, and are sometimes hotly debated by archeologists and anthropologists: are stone carvings of female figures to be understood as goddesses, fertility symbols, or dolls? Very often these earliest works of aesthetic culture may be simply an effusion of joy in creativity, or an expression of grief for the death of loved ones. Some of these objects that we apprehend in an aesthetic mode with our senses and our imagination may have been created for conceptual apprehension as part of what we have called social-political culture. Grave goods in many instances signify not only mourning, but also respect for the social status of the deceased, which would have governed the access to surplus that the deceased enjoyed when alive. Cave paintings relate to the hunt, the source of surplus food, while the Venus of Willendorf and other stone carvings of female figures often appear to be directly related to the physical culture of reproduction, with their layers of fat around the thighs and buttocks to withstand famine or drought and bear healthy children. Baskets and ceramics are containers for food that may be surplus to immediate needs, while clothing may meet the material requirements of physical protection but at the same time offers a canvas for declaring social status, and as such may be part of both aesthetic and social-political culture, denoting social position and control over what is revealed and what is concealed of the human body—traditions with which we are familiar today. Functional objects may be apprehended sensually, and so become part of aesthetic as well as material culture.

Aesthetic culture today is expressed in a wide variety of ways, including:

- The visual and performing arts—painting, sculpture, graphic arts, music, dance, theater, broadcasting, film, and video.
- Literature, such as poetry, drama, novels, and story telling, which appeals to our sensual imagination. Nonfiction books, which are primarily cognitive rather than imaginative, form part of social-political culture, unless their subject matter is one of the sciences or other subjects involved in physical or material culture.
- Architecture of both buildings and landscapes, industrial design, craft, and fashion, which manifest aspects of both aesthetic and material culture, appealing to our senses with visually communicated meanings while also meeting material or physical culture needs.

In the context of our understanding of the four kinds of culture, we can offer a definition of a *work of art*—whether visual, literary, performing, or virtual—*as a manifestation of aesthetic culture in which nature or natural properties are transformed to create meanings that can be apprehended, understood, and appreciated primarily by our senses or our imagination as an extension of our senses.* As philosopher Gilles Deleuze (1925–1995) and psychoanalyst Félix Guattari (1930–1992) put it in their last collaboration, entitled *What Is Philosophy?* (trans. Janis Tomlinson, Columbia University Press, 1994), "The work of art is a being of sensation and nothing else: it exists in itself."

By emphasizing the hermeneutics of how aesthetic culture is apprehended, appreciated, and comprehended sensually, this definition ensures that we do not consider a work of art solely in terms of what our cognitive faculties can understand about it. Attempts at censorship, for example, are usually based on an exclusively cognitive account of the work of art—an undertaking by social-political culture to exert control over aesthetic culture. Simplistic theories of the "relevance" of the arts similarly often focus only on what is deemed to be their social significance.

Works of art carry meanings that are open to multiple interpretations, but these meanings are embedded in sensual form, even when they arise in our imagination, as in the case of literature.

Successful transmission of those meanings depends on their appreciation as well as their creation. It's not only the creation of art that depends on surplus, it's also the appreciation of art. To enjoy art requires time and knowledge beyond what is needed for subsistence. Thus the availability of surplus time conditions both the creation and the appreciation of art. Of course inspiration and appreciation may thrive in conditions of privation and suffering, but only when these conditions permit sufficient time and sustenance to enable the artist or the viewer, reader, or listener to keep her or his attention focused on the work of art.

Imagination is key to the creation and appreciation of art. This remarkable human faculty can best be understood as an extension both of our senses and of our cognitive capacities, and in some cases may be related to our physical condition. Imaginative dream states are part of sleep, or can be induced by drugs or extreme physical and mental states. Drug-induced hallucinations have been an important aspect of some cultures, a deliberate seeking of visions, as in ancient Mesoamerica. A surrealist work of art may rely on dream states for its creation, and some would say that the experience of dream states enhances the enjoyment of surrealist works. A utopian novel appeals to that aspect of our imagination that is an extension of our senses and reaches out as well to the imaginative dimension of our cognitive faculties—the projection of the possibility of a better or different way of life; such a novel partakes of both aesthetic and social-political culture.

This example and many others remind us that even though we have classified them to facilitate our understanding, in life there cannot be a complete separation among the four types of culture. Probably the most positive change we have experienced in our cultural work over the past forty years is the removal of boundaries among intellectual disciplines, between art and science, and among the people working in them. In universities and specialist research institutes, multidisciplinary and interdisciplinary centers, networks, blog or chat groups, and other forms of collaboration significantly enabled by the Internet are supplementing the traditional discipline-based distinctions of political science, fine art, and philosophy. To understand the Renaissance, for example, you need art historians, archaeologists, architectural historians, political scientists, economists, philosophers, archivists, literary scholars, linguists, and more working together. And to understand the Renaissance in Western Europe, you need to understand what was happening in Africa and Asia at the same time.

Museums have been especially focused on a discipline-based approach, mainly because the curator's stock in trade is the identification and authentication of material objects. Starting about twenty years ago, however, a few museums led the way in taking an interdisciplinary approach. In the early 1990s, Britain's Tate Gallery initiated its annual "new hang"—regularly changing the hanging of its entire permanent collection in thematic groups rather than by artistic style, school, country, or historic period, the traditional art historical categories, and then presenting the result with all the fanfare of a new temporary exhibition. Since that time, numerous art galleries and museums have followed suit; Atlanta's High Museum, for instance, met the challenges of its uneven permanent collection by presenting its collection thematically, in relation to the content of the works of art, in galleries dedicated to themes such as "Faith," "Marriage," or "Death." Even the so-called universal museums—museums that possess collections from many disciplines covering a broad sweep of human history, thanks mainly to their being the public recipients of war booty and imperialism—are starting to look at their "civilization" galleries in new ways, recognizing that no "civilization" (by which is usually meant a coherent organization of aesthetic and social-political culture in one place amongst one people for a relatively long period of time) can really be separated from other cultures in the same time period either intellectually or by means of gallery walls. We are now starting (but only starting) to see museums linking peoples and cultures through migration, trade, conflict, work, and the process of knowledge generation, which characterizes all peoples at all times. An early example of reinterpreting some collections of a "universal" museum in an interdisciplinary way was the Silk Road Gallery at the Royal Ontario Museum in Toronto, where then–Chief Textile Curator John Vollmer reorganized the ROM collections of textiles, currency, and other trade objects relating to the cultures found all along that historic route. A recent example is the expansion and reinstallation of Oxford's Ashmolean Museum along thematic lines.

It may seem strange therefore that a book about cultural change is based on definitions that seem to draw boundaries among cultural phenomena. Yet we have found that in an increasingly borderless world, the definitions presented in this chapter—which were at first somewhat vague to us but have become more precise with experience—remain valuable tools for understanding the complexities of human culture, especially of aesthetic culture. The *Revised Nomenclature for Museum Cataloging*, based on a system developed by Robert G. Chenhall and published by the American Association for State and Local History, catalogs all the objects of human culture that museums collect in thousands of entries organized by function. It has proved invaluable for documentation, which is an essential first step to understanding—but to go beyond documentation to analysis and interpretation, particularly to relate the objects in one category to those in another, more comprehensive definitions are needed. The definitions in this book are intended as analytical tools to increase understanding and the capacity for more interdisciplinary endeavors.

One of the strengths of our definition of the work of art as *a manifestation of aesthetic culture in which nature or natural properties are transformed to create meanings that can be apprehended, understood, and appreciated primarily by our senses or our imagination* is that it does not convey approval of a category of objects or experiences called "fine art," nor does it imply a hierarchy of any type. Many of those who have studied art history have been (or are still) taught, either explicitly or implicitly, that certain categories of "fine art" are somehow superior or more important than objects or experiences outside the category. Our definition simply situates works of art specifically as objects or experiences of aesthetic culture, and excludes only those that are more a part of the other types of culture. *Pornography*, for instance, may be distinguished from erotic art because pornographic images or performances (whatever we may think of them and with due respect to variations in quality) are part of physical culture, whereas erotic art is part of aesthetic culture. *Propaganda* may similarly be distinguished from the political intent of some artists like George Grosz (1893–1959), for example, resulting in what is often called "political art," because propaganda is part of social-political culture, whereas political art is part of aesthetic culture. Of course some objects or experiences may partake of both aesthetic and other cultures: a well-designed and beautifully made table forms part of our material culture because it contributes to our basic needs, yet may also be a work of art.

Critical discourse and debate is extremely important in understanding the world—particularly the arts. However the critical world of the arts and art critics often tends to obscure critical discourse by using emotive terms to imply whether or not a work is worthy of attention, good or bad. The term "professional" is frequently employed as a term of approbation—implying that only a full-time paid artist can produce good art. Yet the historical record shows masterpieces by people about whose "professional" standing we know very little. Other terms like "sophisticated," "leading edge," "world class," and "original" similarly often mask more than they reveal. There is a very real need—if we ever hope to understand cultural change—to have a common language of discourse pertaining to how we experience the work, how it was made, how it relates to similar or dissimilar works by that artist or by others, and how we can understand what it means. These critical issues devolve on an understanding of seven terms: content, form, technique, medium, style, subject matter, and function.

The *content* of a work of art is *what it is about—its meanings—as apprehended through our senses and imagination*. This is not to say that content is subjective—it is objective enough, embedded in the work, but subjectively our senses may not grasp it all, or may misinterpret it. The philosophical term "deconstruction" is often used to refer to the process of analyzing the assumptions or preconceptions inherent in our apprehension of the apparent meaning of a work of art in order to reveal its underlying meanings; psychoanalytic and other techniques may also be invoked to probe at latent meaning. In all such undertakings, the artist's intention may or may not be known, and may or may not be decisive in determining what the apparent or latent content of the work is deemed to be. The "intentional fallacy" of assuming that the artist's intention alone determines the meaning is indeed a logical fallacy, but in some cases the artist's intention is decisive. In any case, all of the layers of meaning embedded in the work of art are equally objective.

> *The content of the work of art is the sum of all its layers of meaning, apparent or latent, explicit or implicit.*

The *form* of a work of art is *how this content is realized*—the means by which the content is initially apprehended and appreciated, the specific ways in which it stimulates our senses and imagination. Line, color, and texture are among the formal attributes of paintings; key, tempo, and melody are among those of music. When a play by William Shakespeare (1564–1616) is presented in modern dress, its form may be changed, but its content remains the same—although the new setting, costumes, and interpretation may help us to appreciate latent content that we did not see before. A novel by Charles Dickens (1812–1870) and one by James Joyce (1882–1941) realize their con-

tent through entirely different narrative forms. *Formalism* is the error of con-
centrating on these formal attributes as if they were values in themselves,
when in fact they are simply the essential sensual or imaginative means by
which the content of a work of art is realized.

The *technique* of a work of art is *the method by which the form is
achieved* in order to communicate the content of the work. Two choreographers may share the same balletic technique, but use it to establish completely different form and content in two works of art. Piling up impasto on
a canvas, pressing the pedal on a piano, zooming in or out with a movie
camera, or changing the narrative viewpoint in a novel are all examples of
artists' technique.

The *medium* of a work of art is *the range of techniques* that the artist
chooses to communicate the meaning of his or her work. If the medium is
painting, the technique might be that of a brush or a spatula, and the form
that results from the use of that technique will consist of an arrangement of
color, line, shape, and texture. If the medium is opera, a variety of musical,
costume, make-up, and set design techniques will result in a range of forms
that will include a complex arrangement of sounds, sights, and performances. *Mixed media* works of art are not uncommon today in both visual
and performing arts. When Johann Sebastian Bach (1685–1750) rescored a
harpsichord piece, his *Prelude and Fugue in A Minor* (BWV 894), into the
Concerto in A Minor for Flute, Violin and Clavier (BWV 1044), he was changing the medium, and therefore the range of techniques to be employed in
realizing the content of his music; musicologists sometimes call this Bach's
"parody technique," employed increasingly in the last two decades of his life.

Style may then be understood simply as *form that is common to more
than one work of art*. If we recognize similarities in some aspects of the form
of several works of art, we may associate those characteristics together as a
style. Certain uses of color and the treatment of light, for example, are formal traits that many paintings in the impressionist style have in common.
In the past few centuries artists have initiated and organized themselves—
or have been organized by critics or historians—into groups and schools
based on a common style, and because style is one substrate of content, they
are often based on common content as well. The "impressionists," initially
so called by their detractors, were identified by more sympathetic observers
in terms of their content as "painters of modern life." From the late 1940s
through to the early 1960s, the painterly abstract expressionist art of Paul-
Émile Borduas (1905–1960), Jean-Paul Riopelle (1923–2002), and other
Québécois painters was called "*automatiste*," referring to the apparently auto-

matic movement of brush or palette knife that characterized their style, and was related to the surrealist technique of "automatic writing." But the term also stood for the complex content of a movement of revolt against the cultural and educational domination of the Catholic Church in Québec—which was also expressed in social-political culture as Québec's so-called Quiet Revolution, which began in 1960. All too often, art historians, curators, critics, and reviewers seek to classify artistic movements by identifying common stylistic features, sometimes losing sight of the content of the work. The history of art, properly written and instructed, should *not* be merely the history of style, but should be the history of all aspects of the work of art, grounded in the history of the *content* of works of art.

The first four terms defined above—content, form, technique, and medium—are common to all works of art. The fifth, style, is almost as universal, although perceiving and appreciating it obviously depends on our having experienced other works that share the same stylistic features (or on artists or critics having done us the favor of naming the style themselves). It is possible at least hypothetically to conceive of a single and singular unrelated work of art for which no stylistic associations could be perceived; but for all practical purposes we may say that all five terms may be universally applied to all works of art. The following two terms, which apply to aspects of some works of art, are, however, *not* similarly universal.

Subject matter is limited in application to works of art that are representational, and must be distinguished from content, which is universal. *All works of art have content; only those that are representational also have subject matter, which may be defined as what a work of art represents, if it represents anything.* Content is inherent in all works of art, whereas subject matter is something external to the work of art that is represented in that work. Two paintings of a nude, a horse, or a tree in a field have the same subject matter, but may have very different content. One nude may be an academic study delineating the shape, color, mass, shading, and texture of the body depicted, or a neo-classical study extolling the ideal contours of the body, while the other may be an evocation of the nude's eroticism (the content), or simply a realistic picture of a naked woman. The painting of Napoleon crossing the Alps on his horse (reproduced in chapter 7) by Jacques-Louis David (1748–1825) and the famous expressionist *Blaue Reiter* paintings by Franz Marc (1880–1916) of a blue horse rearing have the same equine subject matter, but very different content. Instrumental music occasionally has subject matter, such as the *1812 Overture* by Pyotr Ilyich Tchaikovsky (1840–1893), the *Grand Canyon Suite* by Ferde Grofé (1892–1972) and many of the impressionistic compositions by Claude Debussy (1862–1918) and Maurice Ravel (1875–1937). Musical styles like the blues can be said to represent the subject by musically re-creating a feeling of despair. Novels, film, and theater on the other hand, normally have subject matter in the narratives they relate; but again it is important to differentiate their subject matter from the content or meaning. The subject matter of *The Castle*, for example, an unfinished late novel by Franz Kafka (1883–1924), is a story of the frustrated attempts of a surveyor applying for entrance to a castle where he wants to work, but the content of the story has to do with alienation, bureaucracy, and modern life. *Mother Courage and Her Children: A Chronicle of the 30 Years War* by Bertolt Brecht (1898–1956) presents Anna Fierling (Mother Courage), an army camp follower, as the subject of this play set in the seventeenth-century Wars of Religion; however, the content of the play has to do with militarization and exploitation, particularly of youth, in Brecht's own time.

All representational works have subject matter, but also have content, which is related to but distinct from their subject matter.

Like subject matter, *function* is another term that is not universal, but is limited to works of art that also have a nonart use in social-political culture or in physical or material culture. An altarpiece has an important religious function; paintings can have decorative functions in palaces, homes, and offices. A well-designed kettle is a work of art, but its function is to boil water. Many of the works of art in what are called the *craft* media—ceramics, textile arts, jewelry, cabinet-making, leatherwork, and the like—have a function, although it is important to note that works of art without function are also produced in many of these media. Photography similarly may have a function, or not. Industrial design and architecture are major disciplines of aesthetic culture that must be evaluated according to functional criteria—how well the building or the designed object serves the purpose for which it has been constructed or manufactured—as well as appreciated sensually as works of art. As with subject matter in representational works, the content of functional works of art may differ widely from their function, as any visit to a fashion show runway will attest. To take an architectural example, the function of Frank Gehry's Museo Guggenheim Bilbao, which opened to the public in 1997, is to display and interpret works of art; its content is related to this museological function, but reaches much farther in significance, both in regard to its importance in architectural history and in the

A classical nude by Jean Auguste Dominique Ingres (1780–1867), *La grande odalisque*, 1819, oil on canvas, 91 x 162 cm (35¾ x 63⅝ in.), Musée du Louvre, Paris. Photo: Thierry Le Mage, Réunion des Musées Nationaux/Art Resource, NY.

context of the Basque country and the city of Bilbao. Our sensual appreciation of what is clearly a great building when considered as aesthetic culture may be tempered by our evaluation of its functional effectiveness.

Such examples remind us that while we have been defining terms for components, taking snapshots of the work of art from different angles, the reality is a dynamic interplay of all of these factors in every aspect of aesthetic culture. Furthermore, because the work of art communicates primarily through our senses, it is likely to be extremely difficult, if not impossible, to convey in words aimed at our cognition—like the words in this book—any one of these features, or their relationship with each other. This difficulty is especially challenging when we try to communicate the content or meanings of the work of art, and is usually more so the greater and more profound the work of art is. Hence philosophical methods such as deconstruction or psychoanalytic analysis may be used to try to reveal the underlying meanings of a work of art in words, and these analyses may be useful, as long as we continue to respect the work of art itself as an inherently sensual phenomenon, the content of which is imbedded in its presentation to our senses or imagination.

It is important to reaffirm that all of the terms described above refer to objective phenomena. The artist or artists involved in the conception, cre-

Same subject, different content: Alice Neel (1900–1984), *Ruth Nude*, 1964, oil on canvas, 101.9 x 121.9 cm (40⅛ x 48 in.), David Zwirner Gallery, New York. Photo: Estate of Alice Neel, courtesy David Zwirner, New York.

ation, or production of the work may not have any clear idea of the content of the work, or the way in which that content is affected by their choice of technique that results in a specific form. We the audience, the readers, or the viewers may be distracted by an unfamiliar style or disturbing subject matter. Yet none of this uncertainty implies that the meaning or content of works of art is merely subjective. On the contrary, our sensual apprehension of the work of art as a dynamic presentation of content is an entirely *objective* phenomenon, dependent on the stimulation that is before us at a given moment in the viewer's life and in history. The artist's intentions may or may not be fulfilled in the work; the content that it communicates objectively is its meaning, no matter the intent. This is true for each one of us, whether we are solitary readers of a poem, or seated in a theater audience. The work of art is objective, its form and content are objective; the only thing that is subjective is the extent to which we can apprehend it. When we allow our senses to be open to the stimulation of the work of art, and educate them to appreciate its forms, the possibilities of its techniques, and the range of its styles, we can participate in a work of art as an objective phenomenon. The true connoisseur of any art form (who used to be called by the French term *amateur*, meaning a true lover of art) is someone who opens and attunes her or his senses in this way. For the work of art is not an object of its creator only, but an interactive object that comes to life only to the extent that it is perceived, understood, and appreciated by its viewer, its reader, its user, or its audience.

Yet our senses and certainly our imaginations are themselves rooted in the society and culture of which we are members. So, as many contemporary philosophers have observed, the content or meaning of a work of art (and of anything else) depends on a range of assumptions and preconceptions about it that we and many others in our society at any given time are likely to share. Deconstructing those meanings, as French cultural theorist Michel Foucault (1926–1984) prescribes, requires us to identify and question those assumptions and preconceptions, thereby revealing latent meanings. For instance, the content of a painting of a female nude may appear superficially to be rooted in the sensual enjoyment of her body, erotic or otherwise; but a feminist deconstruction of that meaning identifies the assumption of the "male gaze" that objectifies the woman's body as an object of male control, thus revealing a latent meaning of the painting. The content of a nineteenth-century European painting of an Orientalist subject may appear to be about the harem or *soukh* that it represents; but deconstruction of its meaning may reveal that it is based on colonialist assumptions of domination and control of the country and the people represented.

Such deconstructions do *not* invalidate the apparent, manifest, or superficial meaning; the content of the work of art is the sum of *all* its meanings, manifest and latent. Thus the painting of the nude continues to convey its surface meaning, even while we recognize its latent meaning as well. In Qatar, the Royal Family has amassed a collection of Orientalist paintings in which they appreciate the technique and the subject matter, which often conveys data of interest about their past not otherwise recorded, while at the same time recognizing the latent meanings based on colonialist assumptions and preconceptions that were so tellingly revealed by the analysis of the late Palestinian scholar Edward Said (1935–2003).

All works of art are created on a complex underpinning of assumptions and preconceptions that condition their meanings, both at the time of their

John Frederick Lewis (1805–1876), *The Reception*, 1873, oil on canvas, 63.5 x 76.3 cm (25 x 30 in.), Yale Center for British Art, Paul Mellon Collection, New Haven, Connecticut. Lewis was a British master of Orientalism who lived in Cairo from 1841 to 1850 and returned to England to turn his Egyptian sketches into paintings, including this one collected by Paul Mellon (1907–1999), who inherited his family's banking fortune and became a famous philanthropist and thoroughbred racehorse owner and breeder. Photo: Bridgeman Art Library.

creation and subsequently when viewed, read, or performed. These assumptions and preconceptions are rooted in the other three types of culture—material, physical, and social-political—and as they change over time, they give rise to changing interpretations of the works of art. This book seeks to identify the principles that govern those changes, not only in the interpretation of works of art, but also in their creation.

The apprehension, appreciation, and understanding of works of art is not a simple matter of expressing our immediate response to it, important as that may be. By insisting on the importance of our sensual apprehension of the work of art, we do not deny the value of analyzing the work and the assumptions or preconceptions underlying it in order to reveal its latent content. Once we are conscious of the latent meanings inherent in the work of art, our sensual apprehension of it should be enhanced—sometimes increasing our enjoyment, at other times making us more critically aware of its latent meanings.

It is also apparent how inherently *social* the meaning or content of a work of art is, since the extent to which its meanings can be grasped at any given time is dependent on our awareness of the underlying assumptions or preconceptions that need to be deconstructed or analyzed in order to reveal its latent meanings—those that were current at the time of its creation, and those that affect our own perception of the work today. When viewing the performance of Shylock in a production of *The Merchant of Venice*, for example, we need to be aware of how Jews were perceived in Shakespeare's time, and how our contemporary awareness of the atrocities made possible by anti-Semitism affect both the actor and his audience. The fact that *The Merchant of Venice* is one of the works of Shakespeare most often taught in schools and performed professionally may also say something about the uses of art.

Such assumptions and preconceptions are rooted in the society within which the work of art is produced, and in the society in which the work is perceived, in both cases arising from the other three areas of culture—material, physical and social-cultural—that condition its initial creation, and/or its subsequent exhibitions, productions, performances, editions, or translations. In order to understand cultural change, therefore, we must fully understand the work of art as a social phenomenon. That is the subject of the following chapter.

CHAPTER 4

All Art Is Social

IN 1993, Barry curated a survey exhibition of young Canadian artists—defined as under thirty years of age—for the London (Ontario) Regional Art Gallery and Museum. It was before the age of jpeg's, so first I looked at thousands of slides or transparencies submitted by hopeful artists, and then I traveled across Canada to the studios of those whose images looked interesting enough to consider for the show. As usual, I found that the selection from the slides led to one studio visit for every thirteen hopeful submittals—an uncanny ratio that I had discovered in earlier selections, including a 1965 show at the New Brunswick Museum of that year's Inuit carvings chosen from all over the Arctic.

The artists I visited for this *Young Contemporaries '93* exhibition were all maintaining studios. Some had day jobs, some had parents supporting them, many were sharing with others, but all had to find a way to rent space in which to work. Several were creating "environments," so they needed larger areas. All had to pay for their materials, a condition that inspired some to improvise. Only a few had even a tentative arrangement with a commercial gallery or dealer, and so had received any revenue from their creative work. About one in three of those visited were selected for the exhibition of three photographers, seven sculptors, and a dozen painters.

Looking back on that survey today, it is interesting to note that one of the young artists, Marla Hlady, has established a reputation for her ingenious concept art. Another, a promising painter, was just beginning to gain some renown through further exhibitions before his untimely death some years later. A third, a young sculptor named Ray Cronin, is now director of a provincial museum, the Art Gallery of Nova Scotia in Halifax. Teresa Marshall has gone on to make memorable films as well as visual art about her identity as a First Nations artist. Laurie Papou, having added multimedia projection to her realistic figure paintings, achieved her first solo exhibition in New York in 2009. Some are still making art today because they are teaching in Canada's art colleges or universities. But others are no longer producing art: the cost of maintaining a studio, buying materials, and affording the time and energy to keep producing work indefinitely became too much for them. They needed a public, certainly, but above all they needed *patronage* in order to keep producing art.

Art is often mistakenly conceived as an individual pursuit. We think of the lonely novelist, or the romantic cliché of the artist or composer working in isolation in his or her studio. In fact, art is always social. The artist produces the work of art with a viewer, a listener, a reader, or an audience in mind. Even in the extreme example of some funerary art, such as a Paracas Necropolis textile in pre-Columbian Peru, woven in great lengths to be wrapped around a corpse and entombed so that it would never be seen again, the meaning of the work—articulated in its iconography—is inherently social because it would be "seen" in the afterlife, which was continuous with the living. Most artists who claim to work only for themselves, like the so-called outsider artists of today working in conditions of extreme isolation, actually imagine an ideal audience, although they may not live to see it.

Aesthetic culture is always created by people working together or alone to produce works of art for an audience, for viewers, clients, or readers. Artists themselves may form groups such as "schools" of artists or movements to develop and advocate for a style, content, or subject matter that the artists have in common. Many art forms, such as theater, ballet, opera, architecture, and filmmaking, require a social organization to produce them. But whether the art form is individualistic or inherently social in its mode of production, works of art are developed by the collaboration of cultural producers with their actual or desiderated audience.

This is obviously true of individual works of art, which can communicate even their apparent meaning (let alone their latent meanings) only when, or to the extent that, those who see them, hear them, or read them can appreciate them. More importantly for an understanding of cultural change, it is also true of a generalized set of meanings of a group of works of art that can be appreciated by an informed audience familiar with the aesthetic culture in which those works of art are produced. When these meanings are generalized over a long period of time in a great many works of art, they illustrate or may become the source of common *meanings* (often referred to as "values" in this context) that may be shared by artist and audience. Taken together, these meanings, when consciously adopted, are said to constitute the core values of a group's culture. We are familiar with the republican and secular values of "French culture," the freewheeling "hippie culture," or the class consciousness of "working-class culture," referring to the values that these groups allegedly share. Even though we are likely to find considerable variation among individuals, these shared values are usually important for many within each group.

There are also many instances when artists and critics have formed groups with common values and have declared a new style or an approach in order to change the culture of society. For example, the Pre-Raphaelites in mid-nineteenth-century England wanted society to return to the values of piety and collectivism that they perceived and admired in the late medieval period prior to Raphael and the Renaissance. Reggae, rap, or hip hop musicians similarly have many values in common.

Almost any group of people will evince some aspects of a common culture—so we may speak of the "corporate culture" of a company or of the employees in a workplace. On a much larger and more significant scale are the cultures of nation-states, generations, regions, or socioeconomic groups. Identifying their cultural characteristics—their values—is important, since it ensures that we do not fall prey to false notions that the differences among them are "racial." On the other hand, it is also necessary to remember that individuals within these groups will vary widely; generalizations about the cultural characteristics of a group should not be applied to all persons within that group, out of respect for the individual differences among them. Nor should any description of a culture be taken as permanent—when in fact we know it is constantly subject to change.

A distinction can also be made as to whether an individual or a group adheres to or identifies with culture "in itself" or "for itself." When culture is accepted *in itself,* we mean that it is merely received; whereas when culture is grasped *for itself,* it is consciously taken up. This concept becomes relevant in the discussion of patronage in chapter 5.

Any individual simultaneously participates in the cultures of various social groups, although some will be more definitive than others for him or her. A young female factory worker in Milan may exemplify Italian culture, youth culture, feminist culture, and working-class culture simultaneously, and at various times one or the other may predominate in her feelings, actions, opinions, and values. Furthermore, all four of those cultures are constantly changing at differing rates, and the young woman's relationship to and participation in them is also in a process of constant change. She may even consciously or unconsciously reject the received cultural characteristics of one or more of the groups to which she belongs and consciously grasp one of those cultures *for itself.*

Appreciating the social dynamics of culture and individuals' participation in it is crucial to our understanding of cultural change. As material culture provides greater surplus for those who have access to it and physical culture generates a greater life expectancy for those who benefit from medical advances, at least some individuals will have more time to produce works of art, while some others will have more time to enjoy them. Those who have learned the appropriate skills—in some societies for many generations through apprenticeships, or by being born into a family of artisans—will be able to refine their techniques, in some cases innovating new styles, exploring new subject matter, and expressing new content. Access to the necessary materials and media is a constraint for some, especially artists of lower socioeconomic class or income, unless they are working in some privately or publicly subsidized art production facility, such as the porcelain factories of China and Europe or the various national or civic theaters.

Opportunities and constraints govern not only the artists who produce the culture's meanings, but also those in the artists' audience who respond to the works of art. People with little free time cannot participate fully in their society's aesthetic culture. Nor can many of those who must use all or most of their energy to provide the basic necessities of life, their material culture. In some societies certain classes or genders may be discouraged, forbidden, or entirely excluded from participation in various art forms, whereas in others the limitations of time, energy, and financial resources effectively constrain the levels of participation for many.

> *The ability of any group of people to generate and participate in a distinctive culture depends on the amount and quality of the resources—time, energy, skills, materials, media—at their disposal. Their patronage as well as their creativity is conditioned by these factors.*

The term "patronage" is most often used in a narrowly misleading way:

- "Patron" in many instances refers strictly to a wealthy individual who provides support to the arts through donations, purchases, or commissions.
- Or "patrons" may be more democratically applied to the larger marketplace, as in "box office patrons" or "movie patrons."

These narrow examples distract us from the full extent of the complex organizations through which societies apply their surplus to support artists and the production of aesthetic culture. While stories of individual patrons are interesting and analyses of attendance and box office statistics have their significance, the great story is how and why societies allocate surplus to ensure that aesthetic culture survives—and sometimes thrives. We need a broader definition of patronage that embraces this wider meaning:

Patronage of the arts is the way that any social group distributes and enables and controls access to the surplus resources available for both the production and the appreciation of aesthetic culture.

As curator of art at the New Brunswick Museum in Saint John in the mid-1960s, Barry enjoyed visiting the home and studio of the distinguished Canadian painter Jack Humphrey (1901–1967). On what was to be my last visit, the artist excitedly took me down to his basement, gestured proudly, and proclaimed "There it is!"

I looked for a painting in the gloom of the cellar, but could see nothing, so I asked "There is what?"

"The new furnace!" he exclaimed. Humphrey lived with his wife Jean in a tiny frame home that had always been inadequately heated by a minimally functioning wood stove. Only now, after more than twenty-five years as a recognized Canadian artist, had he been able to afford an oil furnace. A few years later, shortly after his death, I attended an auction where one of his large abstract paintings sold for more than the cost of several oil furnaces.

Humphrey had established himself as a painter of portraits and landscapes in the 1940s, earning critical acclaim in exhibitions in Montreal and Toronto, but continuing to eke out a living in his Maritime hometown. In 1941, Canada's artists had organized a national conference in Kingston, Ontario, with the aim of stimulating government patronage of the arts, comparable to what the 1930s administration of Franklin Delano Roosevelt (1882–1945) had done in the United States by hiring artists under the Works Progress Administration during the Great Depression. Of course in 1941, World War II had already started two years earlier for Canada, and the war and its aftermath delayed any action, but in 1949 the government responded by appointing Vincent Massey (1887–1967), a distinguished patron himself, to study the need for government patronage of the arts, and on the basis of his report subsequently established a new patronage institution, the Canada Council. In the early 1950s Humphrey had taken advantage of one of its first grants to deepen his understanding of non-representational art and to travel and paint in Europe. By the time Barry met him, he was known as a painter of vigorous abstractions as well as lively figure studies, exhibited regularly with a commercial gallery in Montreal, and was included in most Canadian art survey exhibitions. Yet after a lifetime of creative work, and careful saving by Jean, he could just manage to afford a furnace to heat their home in the last few years of his life.

Humphrey's patronage while he was alive included those who commissioned his early portraits, those who bought paintings from his commercial gallery exhibitions in Montreal, museums like mine that purchased and exhibited his work in retrospectives, and the federal government through the Canada Council. His patrons might also be said to include his wife Jean, who made his meager earnings last, so that he could continue to paint throughout most of his adult life. After his death, the auction houses joined his patronage group.

Only those who possess or gain access to the time, energy, skills, materials, and media of their chosen art forms can become artists, and only those who have or can acquire the necessary time, energy, knowledge, and resources can become patrons. Only those who can keep this access or control over a period of time can continue as artists or patrons. In some social groups certain individuals have greater opportunity to become or continue as artists or patrons, while in others the capacity to participate in the creation or appreciation of culture is extremely difficult or almost impossible to acquire or develop. A society in which a large percentage of the population has the opportunity to become artists and patrons may be said to be more "open" than one in which the number of artists and patrons is constrained because of scarcity of resources or too concentrated a political control over surplus resources: the greater the participation in the creation and appreciation of meanings, the more open and fluid that society will be.

"Creative economy" is a term coming into common use for societies (particularly cities) that have large numbers of both artists and patrons, along with large groups of knowledge workers and knowledge patrons—in our terms the artists and their patrons are working in aesthetic culture, while the knowledge workers and patrons are employed in the social-political cultural sector. It has been persuasively argued by economists like Richard Florida that such cities will be the most successful in the twenty-first century. Florida has shown that in the last twenty years, cities in developed countries have increased knowledge workers as a percentage of the workforce from 10 percent to as much as 45 percent. These numbers are also a measure of deindustrialization and the movement of much of the material culture economy to the developing world. But wherever they are, leaders in the knowledge economy are very likely to become patrons of the arts.

Patronage is the link between the artist and the society in which he or she is producing works of art. It is essential because it provides the artist with the time and support necessary so that he or she can continue working on their art. *"Patronage" refers to any way in which artists are supported so that they can produce more works of art.* It is well known that Vincent van Gogh (1853–1890) sold only one painting during his lifetime. However, this does not mean that Van Gogh lacked patronage. His younger brother Theo (1857–1891), who was a successful art dealer, supported him during much of his full-time painting career, so during that period Theo was his patron. When a writer's life partner goes to work so that the writer can complete a novel or a play, the partner is that writer's main source of patronage. When governments offer grants or prizes to artists, they are becoming patrons of the arts. When a city provides low-cost work-live space for artists or alters its codes to make it more economically feasible for artists to settle in a certain area, the city is a patron. When a filmmaker teaches at a school, that educational institution is his or her source of patronage. When a violinist in the local orchestra earns part of his or her income from teaching private lessons, those students are part of the patronage, not just of that violinist but also for the entire orchestra—since without that supplement the violinist cannot afford to play in the orchestra.

Any individual, organization, or institution that enables an artist or artisan to keep producing works of art is a patron.

In an open society, culture begets more culture. To stay with the previous example, the better the local orchestra and the more recordings it makes, the more students are likely to be attracted to take private lessons from its musicians. In many countries over the past fifty years, the enormous growth in the number of art schools and in the teaching of the arts in colleges and universities has provided patronage to artists and has materially increased the number of artists at work in many media. An interesting by-product of this patronage by educational institutions is that more and more artists have not only a university education, but also advanced degrees. This is the case for a wide range of artists—Hollywood actors, concept artists, jazz musicians, and arts managers alike. Two generations ago, most of these artists would have had only a high school diploma at the most. So the source of

The one painting sold during his lifetime: Vincent van Gogh (1853–1890), *The Red Vineyard at Arles*, 1888, oil on canvas, 73 x 91 cm (28¾ x 35¾ in.), Pushkin Museum of Fine Arts, Moscow. Photo: Erich Lessing/Art Resource, NY.

patronage has an effect on the artists themselves, as well as on the work they produce.

Now we can see how our earlier discovery of the roots of aesthetic culture in the production of and access to surplus is expressed in the inherently social character of the arts:

> *In terms relevant to a dynamic theory of culture, patronage may be defined as the allocation of society's surplus for the production of aesthetic culture. Patronage becomes possible when any individual or social group enjoys sufficient control of the surplus to be able to sustain the production of more than one work by an artist or artisan.*

Hypothetically we may conceive of a person producing an individual work of art for which there might be no need for a patron; but as soon as that person becomes an artist or artisan by deciding to dedicate all or a significant part of his or her time and energy to the production of more works of art in whatever medium, he or she becomes dependent on some form of patronage in order to do so. If the dedication to creation of works of art is full-time, so must be the patronage.

Now we can also see that all art is inherently social in two senses:

- Art is social in the sense that it is produced for an audience of viewers, listeners, or readers, real or imagined, and only communicates its meanings when it is seen, read, or experienced.
- More fundamentally, art is inherently social because the artist or artisan is dependent on a source of patronage to continue producing works of art.

We may thus distinguish between the artist's *public* and his or her source of *patronage*. The public is important, but patronage is more fundamental to the social character of art because the artist is dependent on it in order to produce more than one work of art before he or she finds an audience of sufficient scale so that the market or box office (the public) can become the largest patron. An audience or public for an artist is desirable, but a source of patronage is essential. As the example of Van Gogh suggests, finding the audience may take more than a lifetime. Or it may never happen at all. But without surplus in the economy (remember that Van Gogh's brother was an art dealer), patronage cannot survive and more works of art cannot be produced at all.

Even when an artist or artisan connects with his or her public more quickly, as child prodigy musicians sometimes do, patronage remains critical to sustaining an artist's work and reputation. Once the public is securely won, if the artist is successful, his or her patronage may become identical with the public, the groups or classes of people attracted to buy (or buy tickets to or copies or downloads of) his or her work. Of course if the public's enthusiasms change, the artist or artisan must then find alternate means of patronage—or perhaps find another career.

The preceding examples are taken from within contemporary global society, one in which works of art are treated as commodities, so that the public responds by buying the work in one way or another (purchasing tickets, downloading, or whatever), while the source of patronage enables the artist or artisan to meet his or her material and physical culture needs, so that he or she can dedicate all or most of his or her time and energy to the production of works of art. However, the importance of patronage holds true for all previous societies and for alternative economic systems as well, since there always has to be some support for the artist or artisan to be able to continue producing works of art. In many earlier periods there has been little or no public for works of art in the sense that it is meant today; but there was always patronage—shamanic, royal, papal, priestly, or aristocratic—vital to the artist's ability to continue producing. In socialist society, much of the patronage comes from the state because the state controls most of the surplus.

Understanding the dynamics of patronage, how it works and has worked throughout human history, is essential to comprehending cultural change. The following three chapters explore the history of this dynamism, acknowledge the primary role of the artist in relation to the patron, and then elucidate seven principles of cultural change that regulate relations between the artist or artisan and the source of his or her patronage. Taken together, they show why and how culture changes.

CHAPTER 5

Patronage in Action

IN the caves at Pair-non-Pair in southwestern France, with the help of a guide, we examined the engravings of animals naturalistically depicted on the uneven surfaces of the walls and ceiling so that they take on the shape of the rock surfaces on which they are inscribed. These engravings are usually thought to be instructional (related to the hunt) or religious in function. But we were struck by the positioning of the images on the walls near where archeologists have discovered that the fires burned. We asked the guide to simulate the effect of the dancing light of the fire with his flashlight—it was pure cinema, as the animals appeared to dance and move. Could the function of these etchings have been—entertainment?

South African anthropologist David Lewis-Williams, in his brilliant book, *The Mind in the Cave: Consciousness and the Origin of Art* (Thames & Hudson, 2004) suggests that the great cave paintings of the Upper Paleolithic period (c. 40,000–10,000 BCE) were painted by shamans in altered states of consciousness, possibly induced by rituals of starvation, hallucinogenic substances, dancing, or drumming, with the aim of communicating with the spirits in the rock. The Hall of the Bulls in the caves at Lascaux may be best understood as a theater for the performance of rituals.

It is sometimes thought that patronage appears only in societies with sophisticated systems of distribution for works of art. In fact, patronage as we understand it—*the means by which artists are enabled to produce more works of art*—is a universal phenomenon, and has been essential to artistic production in all societies from the beginning. If aesthetic meanings are to be produced, patronage was and is just as necessary in hunting and gathering societies as in all later cultures. This chapter looks at examples of patronage of all kinds—communal, family, royal, religious, commercial, institutional, and individual—as they have conditioned and responded to what artists have produced from the Paleolithic period to today. Of course there are instances of patrons interfering with or even impeding production of certain works of art, but the fundamental function of patronage is to sustain and support artists' creativity.

For the earliest manifestations of aesthetic culture, patronage may have been communally diffused among all members of a clan—an extended family—in some hunting and gathering band. As these clans developed, they became major patrons, not only in the days of the shamans and their rock art, but also as they recently were—and still are—among the First Nations peoples of Canada's west coast. The subjects of their great works of sculpture were and are the animal symbols of the clans—raven, bear, or eagle, for example. Other carvers made masks that helped dancers dramatize the clans' admonitory tales.

As hunter-gatherers became either pastoralists or agriculturalists, castes began to form around specialized occupations—farmers, merchants, and artisans, for instance. Many West African figures were carved for the ceremonial use of shamans, with masks again telling the stories of the origins of a people or the rationale for social control measures, such as regulations on which individuals or groups may marry others. Anthropologists have shown that some figures that appear erotic to us today actually had the function of shaming transgressors of the rules of mating—such rules being considered important in terms of physical culture. The elders, who would have knowledge of the dangers of mating between certain clans, would be the patrons for such works, being in a position to control access to surplus and exercise social control. It is also known that there are times when the young would challenge such authority. Could the functions of those objects then change?

The transition to agriculture—which is now seen not as a "revolution," but as a more gradual shift in methods of food production—supported a sedentary population, and produced a more or less constant and predictable surplus, at least in its most successful locations such as the valleys of the Nile, Tigris, Euphrates, Indus, Ganges, Yellow, and Yangtze rivers. The greater surplus controlled by sedentary agricultural peoples in these valleys meant that their objects of patronage could be larger and that artists and artisans could specialize not only throughout a lifetime but also over succeeding generations. These river valleys made possible a monoculture of grains, which in turn made those who toiled in the grain fields dependent on others for their own sustenance. The social organization needed to control access to and distribution of this larger and more constant surplus, along with managing those whose labor was needed to produce it, was necessarily more complex than that of most hunting and gathering peoples, usually involving social class differentiation, often including slavery. The highest castes or slave-owning courts and aristocrats typically became the patrons, often along with a priestly class, while artisans and artists usually found themselves in a median or lower social role, sometimes even among the slaves.

The opposite of surplus is scarcity, and when we speak of controlling surplus we need to remember that both are relative terms. Control of scarce resources can be as important as control of surplus. In the Indus valley the early urban civilization that we call Harappan, after one of its well-planned cities, was based on control of access to hoarded supplies of water, a relatively scarce resource. We can see the beginnings of class differentiation within these cities, with some areas obviously enjoying much greater access to stored water than others.

The world's most comprehensive and rigidly enforced caste system was developed later in India, and may or may not be connected to the Indus civilization's incipient social classes. It was led by the Brahmins, followed by the warrior *Kshatriya* caste, merchants and artisans in a median position, then farmers or peasants, and below all of them, the untouchable members of Hindu society, cleaning the latrines. The patronage of the courts and Brahmins, as expressed in palaces and temples and their lavish decoration, is well known. However, each caste in fact patronized a certain level of useful artifacts, stories, song, and dance—even beggars who learned songs to attract donors. The caste system was intended to maintain a static, unchanging society, and for many hundreds of years achieved this aim. Artisans and performers, inheriting their roles and learning their craft from their parents and grandparents, developed a magnificent level of skill and technique. The content typically reinforced the caste system and taught the wisdom of accepting one's role.

The monocultures of Mesopotamia in the Tigris-Euphrates valley required records of stored surplus grain and other commodities, resulting in the creation of a system of writing with a stylus on clay tablets in ancient Sumer. The scribes who wrote these records, as early as the third millennium BCE, were serving a slave-owning patron class of kings, aristocrats, and priests. In ancient Babylon during the reign of Hammurabi (c. 1728–1686 BCE), scribes recorded on a stone tablet 2.4 m (8 ft) tall the world's first systematic code of law, governing transactions of the surplus and all the social relations associated with it. So two of the most important of humanity's cultural attributes—writing and law—sprang from the need to control agricultural surplus.

The pharaohs and priests of ancient Egypt formed a dominant patronage class over thousands of years. Artists and artisans served long apprenticeships, often inheriting the practice of their crafts. The result of their millennia-long relationship was an extremely high standard of craftsmanship and selective use of the finest materials to express the same thematic content of absolute control by the pharaohs, their officials, and their priests of the meaning and process not only of life, but also of death. The Egyptian culture of mummification, pyramids, and luxurious grave goods over thousands of years signified that their society's rulers would have the same absolute power after death as they had exercised in life.

Whereas ancient Egypt was rooted in a broadly based agricultural foundation of cattle and grain throughout the Nile valley, each of the Greek city-states depended on trading throughout the Mediterranean and the Black Sea. Each port offered the specific products of its city or region—oil from olives, wine from grapes—and in consequence, Greece developed a culture that was highly conscious of abstract relationships of equivalence and proportion. The equivalence of so many amphorae of wine for so many bushels of grain, and the further abstraction of a cash equivalent for both became the basis of effective trade. Greek merchants and rulers grasped and codified these equivalences and abstractions, so that abstract relationships of proportionate value became fundamental to their economy. Although they were slave owners, their prosperity also depended on preserving approximate equality of opportunity among those who were eligible to enter into these trading relationships (what today is called "a level playing field"), at least for the male slave-owning traders, implying a respect for and interest in the characteristics of each free man. This introduced a humanist context for the abstract relationships of equivalence and proportion in society, all of which became fundamental to ancient Greek culture, as evidenced in the beginnings of philosophy and geometry, as well as in politics, athletics, poetry, drama, architecture, sculpture, ceramics, and painting.

Ancient Greece thus provides a contrast to Egypt—an example of a slave-holding society in which various forms of oligarchy, and in some cases democracy, among the slave-owners made them a patron group that demanded works of art evoking the beauty of proportions—specifically proportions of the human body, especially in sculpture and architecture. Anyone who sits in the ruins of a classical Greek theater such as Epidauros today immediately senses the attention to human proportion that underlies its architecture and affected the dramas enacted there. Abstract concepts of relationships of equivalence and proportion were equally evidenced in Greek mathematics and philosophy, as opposed to the hieratic principles of slave-owners' religions elsewhere in the ancient world.

Greek artists and artisans formed a median social class more or less respected by their patrons but distinct from them. Another striking instance of the mercantile ancient Greek city-states' concern with proportionate and humanistic relationships was their custom of competitions among poets and dramatists as well as athletes, all of whom were often seen as representing their home cities. Greek comedies and tragedies alike probed issues of justice and fate—posing questions about the proportions of each in all aspects of human life—as they retold the myths of the unequal interaction between their heroes and their all-too-human gods. *Medea* by Euripides (480–406 BCE), for example, considers what should be the proportionate response of a woman betrayed by her husband, as the chorus laments Medea's slaughter of their children.

The Greek city-states established colonies on a similar trading basis to their mother cities, thereby spreading a comparable culture from the Crimean peninsula in the Black Sea to the western Mediterranean. The conquests of Alexander the Great (356–323 BCE) spread Hellenistic culture even farther to the east, but because the regimes that succeeded him had a broader agricultural (often monocultural) basis, instead of exclusive reliance on trade, the focus on human proportion weakened, with increasingly bombastic monuments to the autocratic rulers replacing the measured columns of ancient Athens.

Ancient Rome preserved some aspects of Hellenistic culture—Roman dramatists and philosophers continuing the Greek questioning of what is proportionate in human relations, while sculptors both copied Greek originals and interpreted Greek style in carved stone portrait busts of political and cultural leaders. But beginning with Augustus (63 BCE–14 CE), the dominant imperial patronage of the emperors and slave-owning senators gradually supplanted Greek proportionality with Roman monumentality, splendor, and ultimately decadence. Even before the reign of Augustus, the Roman orator and philosopher Cicero (106–43 BCE) delivered one of the first denunciations of avaricious patrons in his speeches to the Senate, attacking a former governor of Sicily who had abused his position to acquire a rich collection of works of art illegally.

Ancient China provides another outstanding case study in the patronage of an imperial culture. The Great Wall of China is perhaps the most powerful expression of the patronage of a kingdom intent on its survival, not in eternity (like the Egyptians) but in the real world of external threats. The

The ancient Greek sense of human proportion, perfectly realized in the Theater at Epidauros. Photo: Foto Marburg/Art Resource, NY.

first emperor's commissioning of the famous terracotta warriors for his tomb equally demonstrates a quest for eternal dominance. Over thousands of years the Chinese court established centralized patronage even over such applied art forms as ceramics, resulting in the production of works of outstanding quality, emulated in turn by the imperial courts of Korea and Japan.

Successive Chinese dynasties varied the focus of the patronage of the courts and feudal warlords, at times introducing form and content brought to the Heavenly Kingdom by conquering peoples like the Mongols or the Manchu. The architecture of the Forbidden City in Beijing, for example, which was the home of twenty-four emperors through the Ming and Qing dynasties from 1420 to 1911, makes reference to architectural traditions of the earlier Yuan and Sung dynasties, but was derived directly from the Manchu palace in what is now Shenyang, itself modeled on the former military camps of the Manchu invaders who became the Ming emperors.

Just as European patronage responded to the artists' understanding of new developments in the world in styles of architecture and sculpture such as Romanesque and Gothic, so in China the leading patrons favored the artists of each dynasty who defined new directions in the world as they

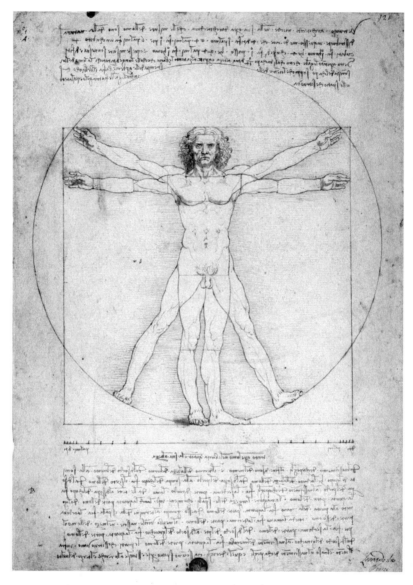

Resuming the culture of human proportion in the Renaissance: Leonardo da Vinci (1452–1519), *Vitruvian Man*, c. 1492, pen and ink, 34.4 x 25.5 cm (13½ x 10 in.), Gallerie dell'Accademia, Venice. *Vitruvian Man* illustrates the proportional canon laid down in Book III of *De Architectura* by the Classical Roman architect Marcus Vitruvius Pollio (c. 80/70 BCE–15 CE+). The text, written in mirror writing, lists the proportional relationships of the many parts of the body that Leonardo took from Vitruvius's canon. Photo: Cameraphoto Arte, Venice/Art Resource, NY.

knew it in their bronze or ceramic sculpture, architecture, and other arts—expressionism in the T'ang, classicism in the Northern and Southern Sung dynasties, and so on. Since the feudal economic base of China did not fundamentally change, the relationship of patronage and artist remained much the same, thereby sustaining a remarkably advanced level of traditional techniques in all media through generations of artists and artisans. *The pace of cultural change varies directly with the rate of change among patron groups.*

In the west, Islamic culture replaced the imperial patronage of Byzantine Rome with that of its own Caliphate, and introduced a new emphasis on abstraction due to its revolutionary dethroning of all pantheons with its reliance on one book as the basis for all approved values. Judaism was the first monotheistic religion of the book, but it was specific to the Hebrew nation; Christianity was more universal, but its book (the New Testament) told a history of events in a specific place; by contrast, the Qu'ran claimed to be simply a record of the Word of God delivered to his messenger Mohammed. It aimed to be independent of specific regional or national cultures, and indeed to convert others by conquest or persuasion or both. The result may be observed in the underlying unity of Islamic art and architecture, despite its multifarious expression throughout the Islamic world, from Cordoba in Spain to Indonesia. Although there are early examples of figuration in Islamic art, its core expression is geometric abstraction and—not surprisingly for a culture of the book—calligraphy.

After humble (and persecuted) beginnings, Christianity became the Byzantine state religion and was transformed by Roman imperial patronage. The church itself became the main patron, in the west initially commissioning Romanesque architecture but then developing the technology to achieve pointed arch forms in the Gothic churches that more fully expressed the spiritual values of the great patron bishops, as well as fulfilling the civic ambitions of the communities in which the cathedrals and churches were raised, or expressing the attributes of a religious order of monks or nuns. In the east, the Orthodox churches and monasteries provided the setting for the patronage by emperors, aristocrats, governors, priests, and merchants of icons and murals depicting the Holy Family and the saints. In both Catholic and Orthodox Europe, women became important patrons, sometimes as queens, countesses, or empresses, but often as abbesses of nunneries with considerable land wealth and the surplus its peasants could produce.

The Italian Renaissance was clearly the result of the rise of a new patron class in the cities of Tuscany and the Veneto, competing with the patronage of the popes and bishops in Rome. Like the cities of ancient Greece, these

Italian city-states competed in trade, exchanging the products of their limited territories for all the necessities of an increasingly urban society. Not surprisingly, the princes of these mercantile Italian states sponsored extensive research in and reclamation of the values of ancient Greek civilization, much of which had fortunately been preserved for them by Arab and Persian scholars. Like the rulers of ancient Greece, these merchant princes patronized a content in Renaissance art that was more humanistic, once again concerned with human proportions, in contrast to the emphasis on the relationship between man and God in the churches.

The art of Michelangelo Buonarroti (1475–1564) and Leonardo da Vinci (1452–1519) responds to both patron groups' interests in their time, in Leonardo's case applying the abstractions of mathematical proportions not only to his representations in painting, but also to his inventions in technology. Leonardo's famous proportional diagram of the human body recaptures and codifies the ancient Greek application of proportional analysis to a humanistic vision of mankind. Both artists made works in the new humanistic spirit for religious and royal patrons as well—Michelangelo for the pope and Leonardo for Francis I, the king of France.

By the late sixteenth century the Protestant Reformation that had begun in Germany caused enormous social division that led to several centuries of religious wars in much of Europe. This is reflected in less concern with classical proportion, and less balanced expression, in what is called "mannerist" painting and sculpture. In Germany and the Low Countries, rich Protestant patrons proceeded to encourage an essentially humanist culture with a strikingly naturalistic art, even when the subject matter was religious, whereas elsewhere in Europe, as the Catholic Church responded with the Counter-Reformation, wealthy patrons both religious and secular sought an art that went further in posing the dialectic of the divine and the natural, expressing the dramatic and transformative imbalance of proportion of the baroque. Michelangelo Merisi da Caravaggio (1573–1610) combined picture sales through a dealer with Vatican cardinals' ecclesiastical commissions of his controversially earthy subject matter with spiritual content. Peter Paul Rubens (1577–1640), Diego Velázquez (1599–1660), and Johann Sebastian Bach (1685–1750) are just a few more of the great artists who sprang from a comparable powerful patronage base, striving to reconcile the resultant contrasting thrusts in baroque forms of music as well as the visual arts. In music, the growing interest in the value of the individual, which was due to the strengthening role of the merchant as a patron class, can be heard in the greater presence of solo instruments in baroque orchestral or chamber music—especially in Bach's scores for solos on the keyboard (clavier or harpsichord), which created a genre that subsequent composers developed into the piano concerto in the later eighteenth and early nineteenth centuries.

Composers and patrons in Florence in the late sixteenth century went much further, inventing a new art form—*opera*—in which for the first time, performers sang monodic recitatives (the precursor of arias) in the "*stile rappresentativo*," expressing individual feelings. Whereas medieval plainsong and Renaissance madrigals were collective art forms sung by a choir, the group of poets and composers known as the *Camerata*, who gathered in the homes of two wealthy Florentine patrons between 1573 and the 1590s, sensed the growing importance of the individual in all aspects of life and conceived the idea that costumed singers could evoke the passions excited by the dramatic tales of the ancient Greek myths that they wanted to tell. One of the two patrons, Jacopo Corsi (1561–1602), had made his money in the wool and silk trade and in banking, but was also an amateur composer himself. He contributed two songs to the world's first opera, originally called a *dramma per musica* and entitled *Dafne*, mostly written by Corsi's friend, Jacopo Peri (1561–1633), and performed in Corsi's home in 1598. Although one of Corsi's songs is the only bit that remains of that first opera, the new art form quickly caught on with artists and patrons, as Peri followed two years later with *Euridice* (1600), now the oldest surviving opera score, coauthored with Peri's rival Giulio Caccini (1551–1618). Royal patronage immediately followed the banker's lead, as Caccini was also commissioned to compose *Il rapimento di Cefalo* (*The Abduction of Cephalus*), performed just three days after the premiere of *Euridice* for the Florentine wedding of Maria de Medici and Henry IV of France. Although the early performances were in private palaces and villas, the first public opera house opened in Venice in 1637, and thirteen years later there were no less than seven such establishments, presenting about fifty new operas every year. These Italian composers and their patrons had changed forever people's notions of what songs could do, as the idea that they express individual feelings has remained a basic assumption of both classical and popular music ever after.

While the church remained paramount in ensuring social control and continued to support the baroque, by the seventeenth century Europe's more independent absolute monarchs had centralized their patronage power in the court. This introduced a demand in more independent states like France for neo-classical works of art that achieved an expression of stasis to convey their monarchs' conviction that the imperial order that they had established within their new nation-states was not only everlasting, but also historically rooted in its classical Roman precursors. The paintings of Nicolas Poussin (1594–1665), the dramas of Pierre Corneille (1606–1684) and Jean Racine (1639–1699), and the establishment of the French national academies for literature, architecture, and the arts all served the court that began in the Louvre but relocated to the glory of Versailles and was emulated by lesser courts throughout continental Europe.

The success of the theater of Molière (1622–1673) at this same time, however, reminds us that the economic power of the nation-states was increasingly arising not from the landowning aristocracy and the royal court, but from merchants in the towns and cities—the bourgeoisie. Molière's comedy *Le Bourgeois Gentilhomme* precisely captures the dichotomy. Bourgeois patronage power could also be seen in the visual arts, in the appearance of naturalistic paintings of figures by the Le Nain brothers, and later in the small but exquisite still life and genre paintings of Jean-Baptiste-Siméon Chardin (1699–1779), suitable to hang in a modest drawing room. An indication of the growing interest of this rising patronage group in individual expression is their heightened enthusiasm for listening to solo instruments distinctive from the rest of the orchestra, the innovation that Bach was developing in baroque musical forms.

In Protestant Holland and England, urban patronage was far stronger. At the end of the sixteenth and beginning of the seventeenth centuries, as the new theatrical art form of opera was being invented in Italy's cities, William Shakespeare (1564–1616) joined with other playwrights, actors, and producers to erect drama theaters and write plays for a diverse audience in the great city of London. The powerful but infinitely subtle characters in his dramas attracted an audience who were steadily conscious of exercising greater control over their own lives. Two generations later in Holland, the world's leading commercial power at the time, the paintings of Rembrandt van Rijn (1606–1669) equally evoked the pathos of the individual, its grandeur and its inherent limitation in the face of death and old age, appealing to the Dutch burghers' focus on personal accomplishment in the context of the Calvinist religion's emphasis on individual accountability. The pathos of personal existence became the content of many of the greatest works of art of this period—Shakespeare's tragic heroes and Rembrandt's self-portraits undoubtedly the most memorable among them.

By the late eighteenth century, patronage by the entrepreneurial class in Britain had nourished the new literary forms that had already emerged on the continent—the newspaper and the novel. The surplus of leisure time available to the bourgeoisie meant that their families—their educated and literate wives and daughters especially—had the education and the opportunity to read, and in some cases to patronize, a whole new group of authors. This new female public and patronage assisted in the success of female literary geniuses like Mary Wollstonecraft Shelley (1797–1851), Jane Austen (1775–1817), and the Bronte sisters, who presented a new sensibility in their subjects and style. By the early nineteenth century, these new patrons, their new readership, and their favorite art forms had spread throughout Europe and its colonies.

In France, the rise of the new patron class of the bourgeoisie had clear demarcations. During the latter years of the *ancien regime*, patronage at Versailles had shifted from the stable neo-classicism of the previous century into indulgences in the rococo—a lighter and more frivolous manner than the baroque. This contrasted with the vigorous rationality and naturalism of the emerging bourgeoisie, expressed in the novels and philosophical tracts of Voltaire (1694–1778) and the essays and plays of Jean-Baptiste Rousseau (1671–1741). Under Louis XVI the court reverted to the neo-classicism that had been the hallmark of the Sun King, Louis XIV—but the content was still typified by history paintings associating the monarchy or the nobility with the classical and biblical world, as an attempt to justify their absolute rule. In France, artists' success was regulated by the Academy's control over entry to its annual salons, where the patronage of the court and the aristocracy were focused, although the exhibitions were also open to the public (effectively to the bourgeoisie), thereby making them a battleground between the old and the new emerging patron groups.

Into this patronage complex Jacques-Louis David (1748–1825) entered with his far more rigorous neo-classicism and new content invoking the alleged virtues of Republican Rome, prior to the subsequent imperial period that was seen as decadent. When the French Revolution broke out in 1789, David joined it wholeheartedly, serving as a deputy and designing pageants for its parades that on one occasion displayed an aristocrat and a peasant on one float, a white and a black man on another, and a man and a woman on still another, in each case simply but eloquently proclaiming their equality. David's painting of *The Death of Marat* (reproduced in chapter 7) has been recognized as the most powerful expression of the emerging patron class during the revolution, depicting with neo-classical grace and nobility the sordid assassination of a revolutionary hero. During the Napoleonic era, David went on to paint the classic portraits of Bonaparte, including his famous depiction of the emperor on horseback surmounting the Alps, with the French army climbing behind him (also reproduced in chapter 7)—a clear statement of his faith in the transformational capacity of France under Napoleon's leadership to bring secular, republican values to continental countries still suffering the remnants of feudalism and obscurantism. Symbolically, David's *Death of Marat* hangs today in the Royal Museum of Fine Arts of Belgium in Brussels, where the artist ended his days in exile after Napoleon's final defeat at Waterloo. Meanwhile in Vienna, at the opposite end of the French expedition, another great artist of the day, Ludwig van Beethoven (1770–1827), although initially attracted by Napoleon's revolutionary spirit, ultimately saw the invasion of Austria simply as French imperialism, and withdrew the dedication to Bonaparte that he had originally intended for his Third ("Eroica"—meaning heroic) Symphony in E flat major (Op. 55).

Industrialization secured the dominance of the bourgeoisie as a patron group. In the first half of the nineteenth century, two stylistic tendencies and a new pattern of patronage could be observed:

- The dominant stylistic tendency was the revolutionary romanticism of painters like Eugène Delacroix (1798–1863), whose *Liberty Leading the People* was strongly associated with the struggle to establish a more complete democracy, especially in France, culminating in the "July Revolution" of 1830, and of poets like Lord (George Gordon) Byron (1788–1824), who joined the Greek struggle for independence from the Ottoman Empire.
- But there was also a more backward-looking romanticism that evoked dreams of a preindustrial era, ranging from ancient Egypt to a fanciful Middle Ages—the latter being most widely expressed in a sequence of Gothic and Romanesque revival schools of architecture, or the novels and poems of Sir Walter Scott (1771–1832).

The new pattern of patronage was the emerging role of women as patrons. Owing to the stranglehold that men still held on society's surplus, including their control of the wealth their wives brought to a marriage, women's patronage was rarely offered in the form of direct commissions and purchases (although further research might show that women's influence was greater than we now realize). It was rather through the *salon* that women provided cultural leadership. Salons were like an "open house," where women—wives, mothers, and daughters alike—facilitated a lively atmosphere (including food and drink) for the exchange of ideas, where artists, philosophers, political theorists, composers, musicians, and scientists could meet. Along with the new scholarly interest in the role of women, there has emerged a significant literature (and some exhibitions) on the role of the salon in stimulating cultural change. Many premieres of major works of chamber music by composers and virtuosos took place in these salons. The popular French writer who published under the pseudonym of George Sand (1804–1876) was both an author and a *salonnière*; Frederic Chopin (1810–1849) composed and performed in her salons many of his greatest works during the eight years after 1838, when he was also one of her lovers. The importance of the salons reminds us that *patronage consists not of financial support alone, but also of paying critical attention and providing the opportunity for influential people to hear or see what the artist can do. There are many ways to make it possible for artists to create more and greater works of art.* The Parisian salon tradition was still an effective means of patronage in the first half of the twentieth century as Gertrude Stein (1874–1946) continued it, entertaining Pablo Picasso (1881–1973) and Ernest Hemingway (1899–1961) and introducing them to each other and to other artists and potential patrons.

By the mid-nineteenth century, the fundamental materialism of the capitalist manufacturing economy resulted in sufficient patronage to support artists like Gustave Courbet (1819–1877), who opposed both of the romanticist stylistic tendencies mentioned above with his radical realism. Courbet, who famously said he could not paint an angel since he had never seen one, introduced a new form of patronage when he opened his own one-man show after having been excluded from the Paris Salon by Napoleon III. Like David, the artist ended his life in exile, in his case due to his enthusiastic participation in the Paris Commune of 1871, the revolutionary uprising of the city's working class. Meanwhile a sequence of French novelists—Stendhal, Balzac, Flaubert, Zola—went progressively further throughout the nineteenth century with realistic novels about the facts of life for all classes of society, while Charles Baudelaire (1821–1867) began an equally impressive succession of French nineteenth-century poets—Paul Verlaine (1844–1896), Arthur Rimbaud (1854–1891), and others—who evoked the emotional life of the alienated individual in modern urban society.

Meanwhile a new patron class had arisen within the bourgeoisie; while earlier capitalists had made their money by manufacturing or trading commodities, this group, who began to become more numerous and prominent in the 1860s, focused on global investments, like the railways. Whereas the commodity capitalists strongly identified with the interests of each of their nation-states, this group had more international interests, because their investments reached out for profit throughout each empire and extended even further around the world. Whereas commodity-manufacturing capital was firmly anchored in the realities of the present

Continuing the *salonnière* tradition in the twentieth century: Man Ray (1890–1976), *Gertrude Stein and Alice B. Toklas in the Atelier at 27 Rue de Fleurus*, 1923, photograph, Yale Collection of American Literature, Beinecke Rare Book and Manuscript Library, Yale University, New Haven, Connecticut. Photo: Stanford G. Gann, Jr., Literary Executor of the Gertrude Stein Estate.

day, investment capital saw profit arising from relatively abstract sources in stock market speculation, share distributions, and speculation on future market conditions.

As this group was gaining capacity to acquire collections of works of art, new patronage opportunities were developed for them, in the form of commercial galleries that offered paintings and sculpture for speculative investment, while the auction houses provided the opportunity to realize profits on their investments in works of art. Durand-Ruel in Paris was one of the leading new galleries of this kind, selling impressionist paintings that were originally greeted as pictures of the present day, but under the influence of the new patronage group became celebrated for the abstraction of specific properties of light and color from landscapes or figure groups. In music similarly, the new patronage sought out composers like Claude Debussy (1862–1918) or

Maurice Ravel (1875–1937) who abstracted certain properties of tone or rhythm to create impressionistic effects.

At the end of the nineteenth and into the beginning of the twentieth century, this investment capitalist patronage grew stronger, encouraging the creation of works of art that focused on specific formal properties—the fierce and arbitrary color of the fauves or the expressionists, the syntax of formal relationships within or among represented objects in cubism—ultimately stimulating the development of a wholly abstract art of color, line, mass, and spatial relationships, achieved by Wassily Kandinsky (1866–1944) in the years just before World War I—the world's first experience of the global warfare that resulted from the fierce competition for profits of these investment capitalists, each ranging for advantage in the resource bases and market places of the world. Kandinsky closely associated his art with the equally abstract atonal music of Arnold Schoenberg (1874–1951), whose compositions inspired some of his paintings.

Discovering abstract art in response to contemporary music: Wassily Kandinsky (1866–1944), *Improvisation 28* (2nd version), 1912, oil on canvas, 111.4 x 162.1 cm (43⅞ x 63⅞ in.), Solomon R. Guggenheim Museum, New York, gift of Solomon R. Guggenheim Founding Collection (37.239). Photo: David Heald, © The Solomon R. Guggenheim Foundation, New York. Painting © Estate of Wassily Kandinsky/ SODRAC (2009).

Of course the other patronage groups did not disappear overnight. There was widespread resistance to most of the new directions in culture. Each successive wave was denounced by one patron group, welcomed by another emerging group, and within a generation justified the investments of those who had been at the cutting edge at the same time as the artists. In retrospect, this pattern can be recognized as one that suited precisely the interests of the new investment capital patron class, and persists to this day. Investment values of paintings rise when the supply of works of a certain period are limited, either by the death of the artist, or by his or her stylistic change; so we begin to hear of Picasso's blue period, rose period, analytic cubism, synthetic cubism, neo-classical period, and so on. The artist does not make the stylistic changes to stimulate investment values, but those values do respond positively to the relative scarcity that the closure of one period and the opening of another induce.

Geographically, the struggle to establish the new art forms was hardest in countries like England where the old commodity capitalist patronage groups had been successful for a longer time. The new direction in art attracted patronage more readily in the countries where investment capital had more of a free rein in establishing its own patronage. Thus even though the artists were French, the Galérie Durand-Ruel found the leading market

Exploring the space of the postwar American *imperium*: Jackson Pollock (1912–1956), *Autumn Rhythm (Number 30)*, 1950, enamel on canvas, 266.7 x 525.8 cm (105 x 207 in.), The Metropolitan Museum of Art, New York, gift of George A. Hearn Fund, 1957 (57.92). Photo: Image © The Metropolitan Museum of Art/Art Resource, NY. Painting © Pollock-Krasner Foundation/SODRAC (2009).

for its impressionist paintings among American collectors, while the investment capitalists of late Czarist Russia were among the most prominent patrons of postimpressionism and subsequent schools through to major paintings by Picasso and Henri Matisse (1869–1964). Futurism, an art that celebrated the abstract values of the machine, found its patrons in Italy and Russia, while expressionism arose in Belgium, Norway, Germany, and Austria. In Great Britain, where the traditional patronage of old manufacturing money held sway far longer, only a very small number of patrons of the arts responded positively to the new art forms, even when British artists created them.

In Russia, the 1917 revolution broke out at a time when the movement toward the new art forms had evolved into a style called constructivism, an undertaking to go beyond both the analytic and synthetic forms of cubism as well as the futurist excitement about speed and technology to create dynamic building blocks of a new social order. The revolution aimed to bring to power a new patron class, the proletariat, and initially the constructivist sculpture of Vladimir Tatlin (1885–1953) and related art forms such as the suprematist paintings of Kasimir Malevich (1878–1935), the free verse poetry of Vladimir Mayakovsky (1893–1930) and a revolutionary constructivist form of physical theater all aspired to earn its support. Within a decade, however, Soviet state patronage began to insist on socialist realism as the most appropriate aesthetic of the proletariat for the visual arts, theater, and literature. Composers who indulged in atonal experiments were denigrated as "cosmopolitan." It was in the new medium of filmmaking that the new state patronage on behalf of the proletariat was most effective, resulting in the masterpieces of early Soviet cinema directed by Sergei Eisenstein (1898–1948), Vsevolod Pudovkin (1893–1953), and others.

World War I also disrupted patronage groups in Western Europe. The group of artists who called their movement "Dada" recognized that the horrendous mechanized global conflict that had resulted from the rivalries of international investment capital invalidated the production of art for this investment capital group. The urinal installed by Marcel Duchamp (1887–1976) in a gallery remains a celebrated symbol of their radical break with the previously held values of art. Ironically, Dadaist works and those of the surrealists who followed them today bring among the highest prices at modern art auctions whenever they are available—proving to certain observers the primacy, some would say supremacy, of patron groups over the artists whose work they support.

Nazi Germany notoriously instituted a dictatorial form of state patronage, ridiculing and forbidding German expressionist or abstract art and atonal music as "degenerate." Due to their virulent anti-Semitism they closed the famous Bauhaus school of modern design and dismissed Jewish architects, artists, and scholars throughout the country, long before launching their "final solution," the Holocaust, in which many Jewish artists and patrons still in Germany (or elsewhere in Nazi-occupied Europe) were murdered among the 6 million Jewish victims. Art collections and other cultural property of Jewish patrons and dealers were acquired by Nazi leaders at low prices in forced sales, confiscated, resold, or destroyed. The damage done to European—indeed world—culture was irreparable. Those few architects, artists, scholars, and patrons who escaped transformed the art of every country to which they fled. Restitution of works of art or their monetary value to the heirs of Jewish artists and patrons has still not been completed, sixty-five years later. And no monetary or cultural value can be placed upon the loss of potential creation.

Until World War II, the School of Paris could claim primacy in the production of the new art forms, with investment capital patrons coming to the French capital's galleries to buy new art, installing it in their homes, and eventually creating great museums, some of which bear their names today. American women, like the Cone sisters of Baltimore, played a decisive role in purchasing the works that form of the core of the great impressionist collections of the fine art museums in Baltimore, Boston, and elsewhere. Another leading American patron who visited the studios and galleries in Paris regularly was Dr. Alfred Barnes (1872–1951), a chemist from working-class origins who made a fortune from the invention of a popular patent medicine, built a great collection of modern and African art in the first half of the twentieth century, and established a unique art education center and museum in the Philadelphia suburb of Merion, where he lived, with a leading role reserved in its governance for an African-American university; his foundation is currently (and controversially, given the provisions of his will) being relocated to Philadelphia's museum district.

The fall of France and the four years of German occupation of Paris put an end to the French capital's hegemony, as both economic and cultural leadership crossed the Atlantic to New York. Stimulated by the surrealists and others who fled to the United States during the war, American artists like Jackson Pollock (1912–1956), Mark Rothko (1903–1970), and Clyfford Still (1904–1980) created a more consistent and confident form of abstract expressionism, going beyond the formal achievement of Kandinsky to produce works on a bigger scale and with an expanded sense of space within which organic color, line, and form take their place. Asserting the worldwide spatial reach of the new American *imperium* after World War II (the spatial reference of the Strategic Air Command), these were the fullest expression yet of the global and abstract values favored by the cosmopolitan investment patron class, and because they were at the same time heroic expressions of each individual artist taking an absolute risk of failure in each painting with these same formal properties, they were also favored by the U.S. State Department in a series of touring exhibitions that were consciously planned to prove to the world America's commitment to freedom of expression, in contrast to the socialist realism patronized by the Soviet Union and other socialist states in the late 1940s, 1950s, and 1960s. In addition to the arms race, the Cold War featured a competition between systems of art patronage.

There was opposition within the American patron groups still rooted in the manufacturing capitalists' old values of representational art, particularly American "regionalism" that evoked the particular qualities of the Midwest, New England, or other areas of the country. A U.S. congressman named George Dondero (1883–1968) opposed the State Department exhibitions, believing that the art that represented the United States should have subject matter that depicted traditional American values, such as the images painted for *Saturday Evening Post* magazine covers by Norman Rockwell (1894–1978).

In the early 1960s, during the "Camelot" years of the administration of President John F. Kennedy (1917–1963), many of the patrons of abstract art turned to a less expressionist, more sublime form of abstract painting called "post-painterly abstraction," expansive color stained into large cool canvases. This may be seen as the high water mark of confidence in an abstract visual language for which dedicated critic Clement Greenberg (1909–1994) claimed universal and ultimate validity.

Yet at the same time, beginning in the late 1950s and into the early 1960s, the gap between the abstract art and music supported by the investment capital patron class for itself and the popular culture of comic books, movies, and radio pop songs that had been provided for general public consumption in itself was bridged by the group known as pop artists. Although superficially their work could be compared to the radical rejection of Dada, in fact it was aimed at creating a major art form of powerful content out of the images of "mass culture." The most perceptive members of the patron group saw the value in this approach, and almost immediately the paintings of Andy Warhol (1928–1987), Roy Lichtenstein (1923–1997), and others were being avidly collected by these individuals and by the museums on whose boards they sat.

The culture of the last fifty years reflects a fascinating diversity of patterns of patronage and creativity. Minimalist artists have taken the premises of abstraction even further to their limit, while conceptual artists have challenged the sensory definition of the work of art advanced in this book by making art that consists principally in an idea that is often more intellectual than visual. Contemporary artists often produce complex mixed-media environments or audio-visual works that are not intended to be seen in a collector's home, so that collectors of contemporary art today very often lease or purchase a warehouse in which to show their collection, even to themselves. Specialized museums of contemporary art feature current developments, striving to provide space for ever larger works in all conceivable media.

Dominant patrons of the visual arts, whose wealth derives from investments or mergers and acquisitions of companies, identify with the entrepreneurial risks taken by artists in this wide-open global art market. French billionaire collector François Pinault, who owns Christie's auction house and many luxury brands, enjoys having as friends the contemporary artists whose work he collects, as he explains in *The Art Newspaper* (No. 206, October 2009): "In the life of an entrepreneur, taking risks are omnipresent, except that in the case of art, emotion is vital, while in business it is generally considered suspect. An art collector also decides things freely for himself." Members of other socioeconomic groups that have less individual freedom of action are clearly less likely to identify with work produced by an entrepreneurial contemporary artist to the same extent or in the same way as an investment capitalist patron like Pinault—a subject that we explore in greater depth in chapter 7.

In China, from 1966 to 1976, the Cultural Revolution was an attempt to establish a new kind of patronage, aimed at replacing the Soviet-style bureaucratic socialist patronage with one that was rooted among the people, especially among students, workers, and peasants. Although it failed, victimizing many dedicated former leaders of the original revolution, beginning in the 1980s the artists who were affected by it began a new, highly conscious, often critical or satirical approach to visual art that has subsequently attracted patrons worldwide. Contemporary Chinese art has become a major force on the world cultural stage.

The art forms of other "emerging countries" in South and West Asia and in Africa are all attracting increasing attention. New communications technologies mean that images are instantly transmitted, so that information about the arts is transmitted globally, and artists today may be fully informed about developments anywhere in the world. Some critics have questioned whether these works of art simply illustrate a new kind of colonialism as they enter the global art market of dealers, art fairs, biennales, auctions, and museums, but for better or worse, patronage, like so much else, has been globalized. Neither New York nor London nor Paris can claim hegemony today, any more than the economies of the countries these cities are in can claim exclusive global control.

One significant change in the patronage of cultural institutions worldwide in recent decades is the spread of "civil society institutions," organizations that are neither government nor corporate in ownership, but part of a growing third sector of the economy called variously the "charitable sector" (in the United Kingdom) or the "not-for-profit sector" in the United States. Until recently, government patronage was the major source of support for institutions such as art museums, state theaters, opera houses, and cultural centers in most countries. Notable exceptions were to be found chiefly in the United States, where a tradition of voluntarism and philanthropy had developed cultural, educational, and health institutions governed by boards representing those individuals, organizations, or corporations that contributed to the establishment and maintenance of the institution in the not-for-profit sector in return for generous tax benefits for their donations. Although these American cultural institutions are often vaguely described as "independent" or even "private," these are misnomers, since in fact they are most often private-public partnerships that provide a way for people of diverse backgrounds to participate as volunteers, giving their time as docents in the education programs or assisting with hospitality, while those individuals or corporations with greater access to surplus wealth have the opportunity to contribute financially to the institutions and to participate in their governance. With adequate policies to ensure that professional staff make the artistic decisions, such institutions can allow civil society in general to participate in them, and can therefore be more deeply involved in the community's social-political culture as well as its aesthetic culture.

In recent years we have seen aspects of this trend toward more involved civil society institutions appearing not only throughout America, but increasingly in Europe and elsewhere. In some cases this is simply due to cutbacks in the level of government support. Even where government funding has remained at previous levels, there has been a movement toward increased public accountability for cultural institutions, requiring them to demonstrate how their public funding is being spent. In the United Kingdom, for example, the government of Margaret Thatcher, Britain's first female prime minister, led the way through the 1980s in requiring public accountability of

Britain's national museums, thereby stimulating a healthy improvement in the quality of revenue-generating visitor services such as retail and food service and enhancing these institutions' interest in finding corporate or other private-sector sponsorship of some of their exhibitions, educational, or other public programs. The Labor Party under Tony Blair's leadership as prime minister (1997–2007) provided policies and funding to expand the focus of cultural institutions from the educated middle classes and tourists to include the working class and marginalized groups such as youth, people of color, the disabled, and the socially disadvantaged. The government's goal was "social inclusion," and one of the key tools was to make admission to the national museums free; but there were many other incentives such as community-based educational activities and creative programs and discounted tickets at the national theaters, including free tickets for youth.

In Paris, the Louvre in the 1990s went still further in reconstituting what had been operated as a government department into an institution that combines earned and contributed revenue with French government support; the Pompidou Center and other leading French cultural institutions are now constituted similarly. The Prado in Madrid and other major European institutions have begun to change in the same direction. A common indication of the trend is that museums and other public cultural institutions gain direct control of their revenues, rather than remitting them to the central government coffers.

Faced with eroding levels of government financial support, many European institutions may have little choice. But understanding the potential of civil society institutions to involve citizens at all levels in their operation and governance, while preserving professional control of artistic decisions, offers an opportunity for the development of museums, theaters, and cultural centers that are more meaningfully integrated in everyday life, rather than functioning only bureaucratically as government services. Because the former government department must now look outside for support—not only financial but also social, since social esteem is the basis for the financial support—the institution becomes a more outward-directed entity, with more links to the community. A good opinion of the institution in the community becomes much more important than it was to the government department—not just for the director's or the curator's professional standing, but also because it is ultimately important financially for the institution to be embraced by a community that understands its value and is proud of its accomplishments. Public programming is likely to be more responsive to economic and social realities, so that the institution genuinely seeks to find ways to be more open to all ages and ethnicities, especially in its education programs. Exhibitions become more of a dialogue with the public, less of a curatorial monologue.

San Francisco's tiny but dynamic Museum of the African Diaspora (MoAD) is an example of a public-private partnership brokered by the City's Redevelopment Agency between the developer of a five-star hotel in which the museum is located and a community based not-for-profit organization that operates the museum. Gail facilitated a planning process that engaged the African-American community in envisioning an idea museum about the African Diaspora. The result was an enhanced understanding of what it means to be African in origin among MoAD's own support groups, as well as in the community at large, extending it to a consciousness of the African origins of all humanity, expressed in the question posed to visitors on a mirror that confronts them as they enter the museum, "When did you first learn that you are from Africa?"

So a more vital type of cultural institution is emerging—a more socially engaged "outside-in" institution that demands new skills from its governance, its management, and its staff, all of whom must be continually involved in training and personal development as the institution becomes as much a learning as a teaching organization. The extent to which this happens depends on the extent to which funding sources become more varied if and as government patronage declines. But enough instances have been observed that the overall direction is clear: civil society cultural institutions are emerging that are becoming more deeply invested in their communities as they work with a plural funding model including earned income, endowments, donations, and sponsorships, as well as the still-important subsidies or grants from all levels of government. More varied sources of patronage make possible a more lively and responsive institution.

Whether the potential of civil society institutions is fully realized or not will be determined in the twenty-first century, in the context of the changing values that we examine further in chapters 8 and 9. This brief and necessarily generalized survey of the history of patronage at work in this chapter is intended to stimulate thinking about the effects of patronage on cultural change, past and present. The following chapter reminds us of the enduring importance of the artist, in anticipation of, as well as in response to, sources of patronage, prior to a more systematic presentation of the principles of cultural change in chapter 7.

CHAPTER 6

Primacy of the Artist

UNIVERSITIES teach courses on the history of important artists, mainly focusing on how the artists developed or fit into particular historical styles. But art history rarely tells the far greater story of how artists create cultural change. That is the subject of this chapter—the primacy of the artist.

In this book when we speak of "artists" or "the artist," we mean creative artists of all kinds—actors, animators, architects, artisans, authors, cabinetmakers, calligraphers, cartoonists, ceramists, choreographers, cinematographers, composers, conceptual artists, dancers, designers, digital artists, dramatists, earth artists, engravers, environmental artists, etchers, filmmakers, goldsmiths, landscape architects, librettists, lithographers, media artists, musicians, novelists, jewelers, painters, performance artists, photographers, playwrights, poets, printmakers, puppeteers, sculptors, short story writers, singers, songwriters, sound artists, textile artists, video artists, weavers, web artists, and any others whom we may have forgotten in this long list. Historically, while many of these artists and artisans in any specific period are known, most are unknown. The unknown include disproportionate numbers of women and people of color, whose contributions are in many cases only now being discovered and acknowledged by a new generation of patrons, critics, and scholars—more and more of whom are themselves women and people of color.

The emphasis in the previous two chapters on the role of patronage in cultural change compensates for the fact that the study of patronage is almost universally neglected not only in much popular discourse on the arts but also in university courses, texts, and museum exhibitions. People often steer away from the subject of patronage because they are afraid of the artist being relegated to a secondary role. Some artists, who merely follow the dictates of patronage, do indeed play a secondary role in cultural change. Others collaborate with their patrons as equals. Frequently the artist is at "arm's length" from the source of patronage, when the relationship is mediated by the market or other institutional forces. But on many occasions the artist plays an *initiating* role, discovering new meanings through his or her life experience and either engaging patrons or financing the works himself or herself. This chapter is devoted to understanding how artists lead cultural change.

The artist Francisco Goya y Lucientes (1746–1828) is inspiring in this regard because he led cultural change and innovated new content throughout his long life. Goya had many different and complex relationships with his patrons, who included both pro-Bourbon and pro-Napoleonic members of the highest levels of the Spanish court, conservative bishops and priests in the church, and Enlightenment reformers (*ilustrados*) both in Spain and in his self-imposed exile toward the end of his life in Bordeaux. Before leaving Spain, he became his own patron, creating a cycle of murals on the interior walls of his home outside Madrid. The house was called "Quinta del Sordo," which means "the Deaf Man's Home," because Goya was deaf when he lived there. The murals depict a wide range of subjects, recapitulating many of the subjects he tackled throughout his career—mythological and biblical scenes, pilgrimages and portraits, and closely observed incidents in the life of ordinary Spaniards. One of the most terrifying is called *Duel with Cudgels*, in which two men are beating each other to death in a vast landscape. These works are stylistically distinctive because they are painted darkly on very black backgrounds. That is why they became known after Goya's death as the "Black Paintings." There is also new content: a profound social critique, and perhaps a loss of faith. *Duel* is a metaphor for the conflicts that continuously tore Spain apart during Goya's lifetime. Goya left few clues as to his intent, but before leaving the house and the murals for Bordeaux (a challenging trip for an old man), he wrote in his notebook: "Who cannot extinguish the fire of his house separates from it."

The Black Paintings were shown in Paris at the *Exposition Universelle* in 1878, thanks to the Franco-German banker and railway financier Baron Frédéric Emile d'Erlanger (1832–1911), the inventor of high-risk bonds for developing countries, who had bought Goya's house and had conserved the paintings by having them transferred with infinite care to canvas. They were greatly admired by some of the impressionists. But these powerful works found no market in France, so in 1880 d'Erlanger and his wife had them

Stuck in a quagmire up to their knees, they are unable to escape each other's blows: Francisco José de Goya y Lucientes (1746–1828), *Duel with Cudgels*, 1819–1823, oil on interior walls of Goya's home, the Quinta del Sordo, transferred to canvas in 1874 by Museo del Prado restorer Salvador Martínez Cubells, with some overpainting due to damage, 123 x 266 cm (48½ x 104¾ in.), Museo del Prado, Madrid. Photo: Erich Lessing/Art Resource, NY.

shipped back to the Prado in Madrid, where they remain to this day. We owe the creation of these remarkable works to Goya, but we owe their preservation and their availability to us today to the patronage of the baron and his wife.

Why artists are at the forefront of cultural change is both obvious and mysterious at the same time. It is often said that the majority of people are fearful of change. When a workplace is reorganized, or a family moves to a new home, fear of change is usually the explanation for the stresses and strains that are evidenced. According to most of their biographies, artists dislike that kind of change as much as the rest of us. But while the rest of us have to focus on tasks that get our work done or our life lived *despite* the change happening around us, creative artists capable of initiating new content focus on the change around them as an integral part of what their work is. Observation, listening, imagining, theorizing, empathizing, experiencing: these are some of the processes of the artist 24 hours a day, 365 days a year. For many of us, these activities are for holidays and weekends, whereas for these creative artists they are the stuff of everyday life. For contemporary British earth artist Richard Long, for example, who began his now famous walks marking his path and picking up stones for his radically simple but powerful sculptures in the mid-1970s, these close observations of changes in the natural environment led to major works that challenge us to appreciate not only the beauty of nature but its fragility due to human intervention. When Goya evoked the horrors of war in early nineteenth-century Spain after the French invasion, he titled one work simply *I Saw This*. Goya—like so many war photographers in our own time—was a witness to terrifying change.

Often these changed conditions will be observed by artists in the art forms that they themselves are practicing—as the formerly disparate group of artists who became known as pop artists toward the end of the 1950s simultaneously perceived on the one hand what they felt to be the limitations of abstract expressionism and on the other, the potential of utilizing the visual vocabulary and syntax of mass culture. Some critics maintain that art is always essentially about art—that new art arises from old art in a closed circle of "art for art's sake." On the contrary, even when the creative artist appears to be responding to a new perception strictly within his or her own art form, he or she is in fact reacting to underlying changes in the material, physical, and social-political world around his or her studio that have affected his or her attitude to or perception of that medium's aesthetic culture. The visual language of movies, television, comic books, and advertisements that inspired the pop artists had indeed established a new economic and social reality worldwide, as prophetically observed by Canadian communications theorist Marshall McLuhan (1911–1980). At the time, a new reality emerged that has continually gained in complexity and significance over the past fifty years, which is why the portraits of Andy Warhol, for instance, continue to present themselves to us as powerful and relevant works today, and why they and other pop art paintings continue to attract patronage.

To take a famous example from classical music, one of the many great accomplishments of Wolfgang Amadeus Mozart (1756–1791) was to transform the meaning of chamber music. Whereas before his time chamber music had been either for entertainment—serenades and *divertimenti*—or for amateurs to perform at home, Mozart made it a means of private and personal expression. Stated in that way, this may appear to be merely a matter of changes within the art form. But when we listen to Mozart's 1787 G Minor Quintet (K 516), and learn from his letters of his anguish about his father's illness and death in Vienna during the months he was composing it in Prague, we can appreciate its consummate, disciplined outpouring of grief and reconciliation, especially if we have also experienced the death of someone we loved. We can also understand that Mozart's transformation of the status of chamber music had to do not with the art form alone, but with finding a way to use the form of chamber music to reveal new personal content in music.

Very often the creative artist who is initiating new content senses changed conditions both within his or her art form and outside it in the material, physical, or social-political world. The late great American choreographer Merce Cunningham (1919–2009), for instance, is said to have combined aspects of ballet with those of modern dance in developing what has been called "the New York School of Dance"—apparently developing art out of art. But Cunningham's choreography did so by integrating movement that he had observed in the way people moved on the streets of the city, movement that had not until then been seen on the dance stage. This opening of dance to contemporary life encouraged him to integrate expressive techniques from the theater, and to conceive and execute dance forms that were sometimes independent of the music that accompanied them. After Cunningham, dance could be about many other things.

Charlie Chaplin (1889–1977) understood that the democratic nature of film as an art form gave him the opportunity to transform his "little tramp" from vaudeville into a universally recognizable character engaged with the devastating changes of modern life—in highly mechanized factories, in street demonstrations, and even in a totalitarian state that strongly resembled Nazi Germany. Norwegian playwright Henrik Ibsen (1828–1906), in the latter years of the nineteenth century, heralded the changing economic and (eventually) political status of women by writing powerful parts for strong women in his plays. Earlier in that century, Charles Baudelaire (1821–1867) sensed the *anomie* of the individual in the modern city and wrote a new kind of poetry that still evokes the contours of urban emotional life today.

Paradoxically, owing to their longstanding "outsider" status, women artists have often been in a pivotal position to recognize and respond to change around them by creating new content. In 1818, Mary Shelley (1797–1851), daughter of the pioneer feminist Mary Wollstonecraft (1759–1797), invented a whole new genre of literature with her novel *Frankenstein,* subtitled *The Modern Prometheus*, which she began writing at the age of eighteen and published when she was still only twenty-one. Writing just a few years before her, Jane Austen (1775–1817) experienced the marginality of women particularly in regard to the male professions in the military and the clergy in her time, and so became one of the most acute observers of the emerging middle class and the changing nature of marriage, from essentially a property arrangement to a relationship of love. Many women artists—from Élisabeth Vigée-Le Brun (1755–1842) to Berthe Morisot (1841–1895)—were restricted to depicting women and children in portraits, but as women themselves were able to see the psychological complexity of their subjects, creating works of great sensitivity far different from the previous representations of women and children either as victims in history paintings, or as the distaff side of family portraits. The great German expressionist Käthe Kollwitz (1867–1945) was one of the most powerful women artists, drawing, etching, and engraving indelible images decrying the waste and violence of war.

The challenges that women artists faced, and in many places continue to face, are only now being identified and fully appreciated. With the rise of feminism, a number of women artists have focused on raising the consciousness of these issues among patrons, artists, and everyone else. In the United States, a group of women artists calling themselves the Guerilla Girls have been particularly effective in calling attention to the systematic way in which women artists have often been excluded from museum collections and exhibitions, effectively eliminating them from most of the history of art.

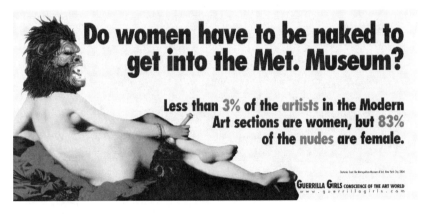

Guerrilla Girls, *Do Women Have to Be Naked to Get into the Met. Museum?*, 1989–2005, poster. Photo: © Guerrilla Girls, Inc., www.guerrillagirls.com.

elles
@centrepompidou
ARTISTES FEMMES DANS LA COLLECTION DU MUSÉE NATIONAL D'ART MODERNE, CENTRE DE CRÉATION INDUSTRIELLE

Answering the Guerrilla Girls' question is the 2009 cover of the exhibition catalogue for elles@centrepompidou, an exhibition featuring entirely works of art by women artists in the collection of the Centre Pompidou, Paris, based on a still from a 2007 audiovisual installation in the exhibition entitled *À la belle étoile* (*Under the Sky*) by Pipilotti Rist. Artwork courtesy the artist and Hauser & Wirth, and Luhring Augustine Gallery, New York. Graphic concept Ch. Beneyton. Photo: Courtesy the artist and Hauser & Wirth and Luhring Augustine. ® Pipilotti Rist/ Collection Centre Pompidou, Conception Graphique Ch. Beneyton; CNAC/MNAM/Dist. Réunion des Musées Nationaux/Art Resource, NY.

A measure of the change in the status of women artists is the opening in 2005 of the Study Centre for Women's Art at the Brooklyn Museum of Art, where the installation *The Dinner Party* by Judy Chicago is on permanent display along with changing exhibitions of art by women and a resource center. In 2009, the Centre Pompidou in Paris reinstalled one huge floor of its permanent collection of modern art so that it consisted only of art by women. This installation demonstrated not only how vital a force women have been in creating modern and contemporary art, but also how the male-dominated world of artists, critics, patrons, and curators created a canon that ignored the full value of this contribution.

Social convention also limited the role of women and people of color in theater and music, which place the individual in public view in a way that literature and the visual arts do not. The emergence of color-blind casting and anonymous auditions in the 1980s provided a fair opportunity for women and people of color to play in symphony orchestras and for people of color to perform in major dramatic or operatic roles not previously considered for nonwhite actors. Original interpretations of classic roles and new interpretations of classical music are among the stimulating results.

As the example of Mozart's chamber music illustrates, the entire history of musical composition abounds with composers who apparently made music out of music, but on analysis prove to have been inspired by changes that they sensed in the world around them that called for a new kind of music. This is equally true of great performers, such as the cellists Pablo Casals (1876–1973) or Yo-Yo Ma, the former deeply incisive in an age of civil and world war, the latter romantically engaged in bridging Central Asian and Western music with his Silk Road Ensemble. Much of blues, jazz, folk, and pop music openly comments on and responds to social change. So does much literature, drama, film, and video art.

Architecture and design, art forms directly engaged with social and material reality, cannot be understood except by reference to their greatest practitioners' awareness of changes in the economic, social, and often political circumstances of their buildings or products. A signal example is the great school of modern design founded by Walter Gropius (1883–1969), the Bauhaus. Established with the patronage of the Weimar Republic in Germany after World War I, the Bauhaus was staffed by Gropius with artists, architects, and designers in all media who were dedicated to experimentation, teaching, and creating useful products that would improve the quality of people's lives and express the new democratic way of life made possible by the defeat in 1918 of the formerly ruling military elite and the emergence of a democratic form of government. Having relocated from Weimar to Dessau (where Gropius designed its signature home) and on to Berlin, where it was directed by another great German architect, Ludwig Mies van der Rohe (1886–1969), the Bauhaus was closed by the Nazis shortly after they came to power. We had the privilege of sleeping one night in the masters' quarters in Bauhaus Dessau, enjoying the unique pleasure of waking in the morning to observe the precise detailing of proportion in the clean lines and clearly stated mass and volume that distinguish Gropius's masterpiece.

So in all arts disciplines and media we have concluded that what appears superficially to be "art for art's sake" almost always turns out to be art that arises from the artists' engagement with the world around them, whether they discover this new content in terms of their own art form, or more directly in contact with the material, physical, or social-political culture of their time and place. This is equally true of art in the non-Western world, and the art of earlier historical periods. Chinese ink painting, for example, is often seen as a highly traditional art form—yet its history is marked by a long line of idiosyncratic individualists, some painting in ways influenced by earlier artists, others developing new forms of calligraphy, still others radically simplifying the brush strokes needed to depict a landscape or the branch of a tree. But all are freshly engaged in establishing new content in their work based on their awareness and experience of the world around them. Or consider the radicalism of the architect and stained glass artists and church patron who conceived of Sainte-Chapelle in Paris in the 1240s, daring to build a chapel in which all walls to the very great height that Gothic engineering could take them would be filled entirely with glorious stained glass, linking the biblical story with the then current events of the reign of Louis IX. In classical theater, each of the ancient Greek dramas can be seen as striking out in new directions related to contemporary life of the time, told through the medium of mythology.

It is also true that there are periods and art forms in which there is little or no cultural change. As we noted in the previous chapter, the pace of cultural change varies with the rate of change among patron groups, so if a slave-owning or feudal economic system can be sustained with little structural alteration over centuries, cultural change is likely to be minimal. Chinese opera, for instance, is an art form that for many centuries within each of its regional variants—Beijing Opera, Cantonese Opera, and others—required its performers to duplicate exactly an "ideal" way of singing the librettos of a fixed canon of operas, accompanied by specific movements and gestures, in costume and makeup that precisely copied those prescribed for each character. Even in this tightly controlled discipline, however, in the late nineteenth and early twentieth centuries there was an incipient movement toward incorporating subtle signs of personal expression—a cultural change responding to Western influences that came as a result of the concessions wrung from China after its defeat in the Opium Wars. During the Cultural Revolution (beginning in 1966) the new patron—the Chinese Communist government of the People's Republic—proscribed traditional Chinese Opera in favor of new revolutionary opera and ballet forms that were widely distributed in films like *The White Haired Girl*. Since the end of the Cultural Revolution in 1976, there has been a gradual revival of Chinese Opera and other traditional art forms, including Chinese ink brush painting, which is widely practiced today by both amateurs and professionals.

Other societies, especially ancient ones where pharaohs or kings depended on maintaining a rigid social order, have endeavored to resist cultural change. Many aspects of ancient Egyptian culture remained unchanged through each of the Old, Middle, and New Kingdoms for centuries. Even there, however, the famous but brief intervention of the young eighteenth dynasty pharaoh Akhenaton (1380–1362 BCE) in religious life is marked by sculptors responding with a new note of naturalism in their representations of him and his court. And of course each of the pyramids and temples throughout the 3,000 years of ancient Egyptian history marked significant new developments of technology and in some cases of the ideology that accompanied them.

Museum storage rooms are laboratories for studying the phenomenon of cultural change. They amass large collections of artifacts, works of art, or natural specimens and organize them by geography, by period, or by a specific site. Having had the privilege of visiting hundreds of museum storage areas accompanied by their curators and scholars, we have seen that although there are societies where for long periods of time there was resistance to change in all four cultural domains—material, physical, and social-political, as well as aesthetic—most art forms reward close examination by revealing the process of cultural change over time in terms of the artists' engagement with what was new in their world.

The commitment of artists and artisans to initiating new content based on their awareness of new conditions in the world is a remarkably widespread phenomenon, even in societies where one might least expect it. In 2001, the Nobel prize–winning Turkish author Orhan Pamuk created a mystery novel, *My Name Is Red*, around the dynamic of cultural stasis and change among artisans and artists in the Ottoman court in Istanbul during the sixteenth century. For hundreds of years the Ottomans ruled a successful empire, during which time their sultans were patrons of some of the greatest artists and artisans in the world, as can be seen from the collections of the Topkapi Palace in Istanbul. At issue in the novel is the use of perspective, brought to the east by Venetian and French artists. Some of the Turkish artists want to try it despite its prohibition by their patrons (who had actually collected a few such works in secret). Perspective was seen by the sultan and his court as a dangerous democratic form that organizes the figures in the picture plane according to where they would stand in observed nature. The rulers preferred the hieratic style (characteristic of most dynastically ruled societies) in which figures remain the same and are depicted in order of social importance, not mere appearance. There is a sense in which this book and others by Pamuk are metaphors for the current situation in Turkey, in which conflicting ideas of social-political change between Westernization and Islamic fundamentalism are at a boiling point. Thus Pamuk writes about historical cultural change to engage his novels in cultural change today.

A glance back at the definitions of the work of art and its components in chapter 3 reminds us that this initiating role for artists in introducing cultural change is a matter of creating new *content*, not merely new style, as is so often claimed. In many instances, the artist's struggle to achieve new content obliges him or her to develop new *forms* to communicate the new meanings. Form is the sensually apprehended means by which content is communicated. When the individual or a group of artists together achieve this new content in a sufficient number of works, common elements of the new form are recognized as a *style*, as happened repeatedly in the late nineteenth and early twentieth century, from impressionism through to surrealism in painting, film, music, dance, and theater. Historians and critics who are following only the succession of works of art in isolation may then hail the individuals or the group responsible as inventors of a new style, whereas in fact the artists involved have sensed new conditions and therefore communicated new content in their work, which has occasioned the need for the new style.

Thus the impressionists were originally seen, both positively and negatively, as "painters of the modern age." They were keenly aware of the disjunction between the everyday world of France in the second half of the nineteenth century and not just the subject matter but also and more significantly the *values* of the paintings that dominated the annual Paris Salon. Following the example of the Barbizon landscape painters and Eugène Boudin (1824–1898), they turned to painting light and color as they saw it *en plein air* (outdoors), or in the case of Edgar Degas (1834–1917) depicted the world of the ballet and the racecourse as they found them. The mid-nineteenth-century invention of photography, which had little impact on salon painting, affected the impressionists directly in their handling of light and in their compositions. These and other influences resulted in a recognizable new style, but it was made possible and necessary because these artists were reaching for a way to communicate a new sense of being in the world.

Paul Cézanne (1839–1906), who had been one of them, wanted to go further, not only to reflect these new conditions, but also to paint something "more solid," as he once put it, something that could take its place in the museums alongside neo-classical works like the great paintings of Nicolas Poussin (1594–1665). His subsequent paintings unveil a dramatic awareness of modeling, composition, and structure, not only in subjects like portraits or still life, but even more powerfully in his famous landscapes of his native region, his pictures of Mont Sainte-Victoire seen from a distance, with its

An unfinished painting reveals the artist's process as he probes multiple viewpoints: Paul Cézanne (1839–1906), *Nature morte à la cruche* (*Still Life with Water Jug*), c. 1892–1893, oil on canvas, 53 x 71 cm (20¾ x 28 in.), Tate, London, bequeathed by C. Frank Stoop, 1933 (N04725). Photo: © Tate, London 2010.

Just sixteen years later, a Cubist still life analyzes multiple viewpoints, structure, and spatial relationships: Pablo Picasso (1881–1973), *Still Life with Liqueur Bottle*, 1909, oil on canvas, 81.6 x 65.4 cm (32⅛ x 25¾ in.), Museum of Modern Art, New York, gift of Mrs. Simon Guggenheim Fund. Photo: © Museum of Modern Art/Licensed by SCALA/Art Resource, NY.

three-dimensional solidity and volume as apparent as its two-dimensional role in the picture plane, all simultaneously grasped with the sensitivity to color and light that Cézanne had maintained from his impressionist period, sometimes contrasted with the delicate branch of a tree reaching across the foreground. The result is a style that art historians have labeled "postimpressionism," and identified as a precursor to early twentieth-century cubism, which develops Cézanne's structural vision more systematically, using the underlying structural geometry as a new visual language to depict the world of interrelated space and time that Albert Einstein (1879–1955) and other physicists were analyzing at the same moment. To describe any of these developments merely as changes in style is to miss the point of each one: any genuinely new style always announces the discovery of new content, in these instances a new sense of space and relationships among objects in the world.

It is most important to observe that the new content is always expressed sensually and imaginatively in the works of art themselves, and can never be stated adequately in a few—or even many—descriptive words (notwithstanding our attempts to summarize them here). In many, probably in most cases, visual and performing artists are not able to state in words or concepts what their apprehension of the new conditions precisely is; many would not even understand the question. Writers are often more articulate, although even in those instances it is much more effective, exciting, and convincing to grasp, say, the new Russia emerging around Leo Tolstoy (1828–1910) in the pages of *Anna Karenina* (first published in 1878), rather than reading Tolstoy's philosophizing about his own work. Even when there is some congruence between what an artist says about his or her work and the works of art themselves, it is important to beware of the "intentional fallacy"—to remember that the content of a work of art is the sum total of all of its meanings, which very often exceed or may be completely unrelated to its author's intentions.

Nor should we confuse the initiation of new content with the creation of new subject matter. In some cases, as in the impressionists' paintings of modern life, new subject matter is part of the story; but in many others, as with Cézanne turning back to traditional subjects of still life, portraits, and landscapes, it is not. The mere introduction of new subject matter does not in itself constitute the creation of new content. And for Wassily Kandinsky and Jackson Pollock, their response to the changes in the world that they sensed around them required precisely their transcendence over (or at least rejection of) subject matter.

Some cultural historians, such as the Canadian literary critic Northrop Frye (1912–1991), maintain that in creating their new works artists are simply recasting classical archetypes. Some hold that there are a fixed number of themes that are continually recycled and reconsidered by the artists of every age. Others maintain that certain stylistic orientations—classicism, romanticism, then neo-classicism again—eternally recur. It is easy to miss new content when that content is accompanied by a major change in style—especially if the critic or viewer looks at works in isolation from the time in which they were created. The stories portrayed in paintings of the early Italian Renaissance are the agreed biblical canon—according to the church patrons or the rising middle class that was commissioning works to be installed in the church. But the use of perspective is far more than a stylistic change. As the contemporary Ottomans knew, perspective organizes the figures as they appear in nature, not as they exist in the feudal order of the world. Representing biblical stories in the fully dimensioned Renaissance square expressed the new content of Italian town life, which was more open and "democratic" than in the monasteries or the countryside. Perspectival painting was created by artists who were aware of the new ways for people to relate to each other made possible by modern and urban planning and design.

Meanwhile, because of the centralization and stability of the Ottoman Empire there was very little change in subject or style of the hunting and court scenes there. Indeed many of the Ottoman rulers look much alike. That was the point of stability. From the twelfth to the fifteenth century in Italy, by contrast, there was enormous change as artists and artisans moved to the new cities and embarked on a very different way of life. This new content is realized in paintings, frescoes, and sculpture even though the subjects remain the same. In the seventeenth century Rembrandt van Rijn (1606–1669) represented some of the same subjects; new layers of meaning are more apparent to us because Rembrandt was living in a capitalist society more like our own where the role of the individual and the importance of character and personality had a determining effect on economic success—something we still believe today! Rembrandt's new content is human psychology; his biblical scenes are intense character studies, as are of course his numerous self-portraits, commissioned portraits, and history paintings. This new content was sparked by close observation of the people around him, who would all have been affected by the innovative and ruthless Dutch business class that was transforming the world through its aggressive mercantile system.

Of course no two artists are likely to be equally inspired, dedicated, skilled, subtle, or effective in communicating new content. Many will follow, only a few will lead. In every historical period, including the present, there have been and are artists of all media—including some well-known names—whose work can be seen as nothing but a response to the available patronage. Many painters in nineteenth-century France and England, for example, produced huge pictures with classical, Orientalist, or biblical themes in order to garner as much space as possible on the walls of the annual salon exhibitions; their works—visible today in some galleries of the *Musée du Quai d'Orsay* in Paris—were much larger than many of the impressionist pictures that now hang in other galleries of the same museum, but the academic works visibly lack the inspiration, insight, and revelation of the impressionist pictures.

It is worth noting, however, that there is a resurgent appreciation of academic art these days—not so much for its content, but because of its subject matter. The French Academy rated history painting as the most important subject matter for the artist. Freed from the conventions of church and monarchy, history painting became an opportunity to explore different peoples and civilizations, which were much more in public consciousness as the economic benefits of colonialism and global trade were brought to great cities like Paris and London and displayed in "universal exhibitions." As a result, artists experienced a world of greater variety and depicted it in history painting where women and non-Western people are represented not always as "objects of history" or "supplicants," but sometimes in active roles. These subjects are especially valued today as we have come to appreciate how few representations there are of women and people of color in many Western galleries and museums. For collectors and the rising new patron groups in the Arabian Gulf, Orientalist works are prized not so much for their content, which is often frankly colonizing, but for their subject matter, which likely contains the most accurate visual depictions they have of a way of life that was only partially captured in photography (and that mainly in black and white), and was rarely depicted by their own artists and artisans because of religious prohibitions and social conventions. Thus for the patrons of these works today, subject matter is more important than either the manifest or the latent content created by their artists.

In general, however, understanding cultural change means understanding the centrality of the creative artist who initiates new content, and how he or she differs from highly skilled artists who mainly follow. Western art museums make this easy because they highlight the "greats" and present the "not-so-greats" as background. "Connoisseurship," a term that has fallen out of favor in some places, is the skill developed over many years to distinguish between the greats and the not-so-greats, and to authenticate works; at his or her best the connoisseur should be able to identify the ini-

Henri Gervex (1852–1929), *A Session of the Painting Jury at the Salon des Artistes Français*, c. 1883, oil on canvas, 299 x 419 cm (117½ x 165 in.), Musée d'Orsay, Paris. A huge painting that would take lots of wall space at the Salon, including portraits of several of the leading artists of the day. Photo: Réunion des Musées Nationaux/Art Resource, NY.

tiating artist and differentiate him or her from the followers. But often the canon that connoisseurs have developed (and it too is influenced by market forces and patronage) overlooks new ideas and creative talent. So a visit to a museum, a concert, a play, the movies, or the Internet is always an opportunity to discover or recover new content and the creative artists who initiate it. This is equally true of innovative interpretations in new performances of the classics.

 Critics often play a significant role in bringing the accomplishment of the creative, initiating artist to the attention of potential patrons. In all societies people have written or talked about art, but in the past few centuries especially, critics attained a new level of importance in the process of cultural change. John Ruskin (1819–1900), for instance, was instrumental in establishing the importance of the great British landscape artist Joseph Mallord William Turner (1775–1851), and became equally famous for attacking *Nocturne in Black and Gold: The Falling Rocket*, an 1875 painting by the American expatriate painter James Abbott McNeill Whistler (1834–1903); today we appreciate both artists and recognize that they represented different stages in the development of the art that was discovering a new world and appealing to the new investment capitalist group of patrons. In mid-twentieth-century New York, critics Harold Rosenberg (1906–1978) and Clement Greenberg (1909–1994) offered differing interpretations—the first broadly existentialist, the second narrowly formalist—of abstract expressionism, in either case supporting the patronage that was crucial to its development in the decade and a half following World War II.

In nineteenth-century Paris and twentieth-century London and New York especially, newspaper theater critics attained great power, as actors, directors, and especially producers of West End or Broadway shows anxiously awaited their overnight reviews of a premiere. The patronage had already been invested in the production costs, but a favorable or unfavorable review could determine whether the public would buy tickets, and so whether there would be sufficient returns on the patrons' investment to continue the production for a long run. Film critics have also been influential, although their effect is necessarily somewhat more diffuse. The Internet has considerably eroded the power and position of criticism of all kinds, as blogs by pleased or displeased members of the audience tend to democratize all commentary on the arts.

The Internet also provides formerly unimaginable opportunities for artists in all media (especially music), to distribute their works to an enormous public, and to find patronage that shares an interest in or experience of new content. The Internet accelerates cultural change by lowering the cost of distribution, breaking down institutional barriers and borders, and opening up opportunities for artists to connect with other artists and with patrons on a similar path. Young singers and bands with a webcam can now develop an international public well in advance of having to cope with the patronage involved in a concert tour or a recording.

Both innovative and imitative artists have crucial relationships with patronage—but those who lead *initiate* the relationship through greater risk-taking, by the capacity (usually in their older years) to self-finance new works, or by cultivating a more "cutting edge" patron, whereas those who follow are content to attract the readily available patronage, the "low hanging fruit." As already noted, this difference is not limited to relatively recent art history, during which we have privileged "originality." Although there have been societies that depended on stasis for their survival and therefore resisted or denied the possibility of cultural change, we can observe the difference between initiating creative artists and followers throughout much of the history of what we today call art, craft, design, or architecture, and throughout literature and the performing arts as well—the entire corpus of aesthetic culture.

The originating or *initiating* creative visual, literary, or performing artist of any historical period is distinguished by his or her observation of something *new*—some new reality, or new way of considering the world that he or she commits to and risks time and materials to express, because he or she believes it is important. The career of that artist may become a lifelong struggle to create that new content—Cézanne toward the end of his life said that only occasionally had he come close to what he wanted to do—or the artist may relatively quickly come to a realization of new content and then vary the presentation of it or go on to further discoveries throughout his career. Think of Picasso, who when asked what he was seeking in his painting replied, "I do not seek, I find."

Difficult or relatively easy, what these initiating artists do is to establish contact with new content, reflecting some new reality, some new conditions of life. These new conditions are emerging in the world around them, sometimes in nature but more usually in the material, physical, or social-political culture of their time. Very often these new conditions are perceived by the artist in terms of their own artistic medium or discipline, so that they appear (possibly even to themselves) to be wanting to change only their own art form, whereas in reality they are responding to changes in all four types of culture. If their perception, however inchoate it may be to them and to others, is accurate and profound, there will be patrons who will respond to it, sometimes immediately, often only after some time, perhaps even after the artist's death. The patrons recognize the new content—not as a concept, but sensually and through their imagination, often without being able to articulate it at the time—because they themselves are living in the new material, physical, and social-political conditions that the artist has sensed, and those new conditions matter to them. Their patronage, early or late, establishes the new works of art, and the new subject matter, forms, or style that may accompany the new content. Lesser artists who are followers may then respond to the new patronage and develop works to meet the new demand. Cultural change has occurred. The sequence goes something like this:

1. An artist or a group of artists, working in one or many media or disciplines, senses new conditions in the world around them. They or others may conceive of their awareness of new conditions as a response to

what they perceive as limitations of their own medium or discipline (architecture, design, music, literature, painting, theater, dance, or whatever), but the new conditions that they sense as possibilities within their own aesthetic culture are rooted in changed conditions in the other types of culture—material, physical, or social-political.

2. The artist or group of artists creates new works in which the new content is expressed sensually or imaginatively. Sometimes these works of art represent new subject matter, sometimes they are presented in a new style, but always and essentially they offer new content.

3. Sooner or later, people, governments, or institutions with surplus resources to expend (patrons), possibly encouraged by perceptive critics, recognize the value of the new works of art because of their new content, since the patrons are themselves living in the real world in which these new conditions are affecting them and matter to them. The new works appeal to them for this reason, and they purchase the works, buy tickets, or support them with grants and subsidies—or hire the artists to teach in their schools. Even a small amount of support enables the artist to make additional works. Cultural change has begun.

4. When the works are off the drawing board, out of the studio and into the cinema, concert hall, theater, bookstore, or gallery, or increasingly today onto the Internet, more people experience them. Some may enlarge the patronage base; others may apply the experience to their work (another art form, or teaching, or scientific investigation, or philosophy). The work might grow or it might just die, but if its new content is being experienced by patrons who can respond to it, eventually it will live. Goya's Black Paintings influenced some of the impressionists fifty years after they were painted. Goya, who was an active participant in the Spanish version of the great movement of social-political cultural change called the Enlightenment, became one of the innovators of a cultural change called "modernism" that is still part of the cultural world in which we are now living.

5. Other artists working in the same discipline or medium become aware of the new patronage available, and begin to create work that is comparable, in form, style, or subject matter. They may or may not be able to perceive the new content, and may or may not be successful in communicating it if they do. They may be more successful than the initiating artist was in finding the new patronage, or not. If and as they do, they help to establish the new horizon of cultural change.

When we speak of the artist in the preceding sequence we mean all artists in all media and disciplines historically as well as today. And when we speak of patronage, we mean all forms of patronage, historical and contemporary—royal, aristocratic, papal, ecclesiastical, governmental, institutional, mercantile, and mass patronage; patronage provided by universities, countries, cities, and corporations, as well as by the artist's parents or partner. Although the kings and pharaohs of some societies have resisted or rejected cultural change, other monarchs—like Frederick the Great (1712–1786) in Prussia or Catherine the Great (1729–1796) in Russia—have played an active patron's role in the process of cultural change. So have the government grants, the teaching jobs at art schools, or the spouse's work in a local factory. While the preceding chapter traced the history of patronage at work, and this chapter has emphasized the primacy of the artist in the process of cultural change, our next chapter analyzes the *principles* that have governed the complex transactions between artists and patrons throughout human history—principles that are still at work today.

Seven Principles of Cultural Change

THUS far we have proposed a definition of culture, situating aesthetic culture among the other three large categories of culture—material, physical, and social-political. We have defined the work of art and its interrelated components. We have reviewed the key role of patronage in fueling this dynamic process of change, and have described how creative artists and artisans initiate cultural change. In keeping with the goal of this book to provide tools for understanding and participating in cultural change, this chapter summarizes our ideas in the form of seven useful and (hopefully) memorable principles.

EACH SOCIAL GROUP HAS ITS OWN CULTURE

The term "social group" may refer to an entire socioeconomic class or a stratum within that class, or more specifically to a generation, a gender, those working in a certain trade or profession, a nation, immigrants from a common place of origin, or people who share the same religion or language or sexual orientation. *A social group is any number of people who are sufficiently identified to themselves and to each other that they have a common way of speaking about their identity, and generate a culture of which they are more or less conscious.* Aspects of this culture could be as basic as a style of clothing, or as elaborate as a fully developed literary and visual form—such as romanticism.

Today most people participate simultaneously in multiple social groups—as in the example in chapter 4 of a young female factory worker in Milan who may be a part of youth culture, Italian culture, feminist culture, and working-class culture all at the same time, or may choose to withdraw from, modify, or reject one or all of these cultures if she chooses. Of course people in isolated or closed societies may not have much choice—especially women in societies where their movements and contacts with others are limited by religious or cultural constraints. In general, however, awareness of the diversity of social groups and their cultures is greatly enhanced by the concentration of people in cities and by the access provided by the Internet, particularly through social media. The cultural identity of each social group is a building block of cultural change.

Our simple but essential first principle is: *all social groups have a culture.*

Not every individual in a social group embraces every aspect of that culture, but each identifies with it enough to be consciously part of that social group; or they may disagree enough to reject it—in some cases even rejecting such powerful traditional affiliations as religion, ethnicity, and social class, or forming another group based on common opposition to the values of the group they are rejecting. But in any case, all social groups have a culture.

Social groups that control enough surplus of time or material resources to support a distinctive aesthetic culture—music, craft, fashion, fine art, architecture, story telling, and so on—have a greater sense of identity and cohesion than those that do not expend as much of their surplus on aesthetic culture. This is a key point: for a group to have consciousness "for itself" requires a more fully elaborated system of group signifiers. The stronger the culture, the stronger the group, and the stronger their identity.

Any group of people will have access to some level of surplus, even if minimal, and will to that extent be enabled to sustain its own aesthetic culture. Even in subsistence economies like that of the traditional Inuit, for instance, we can recognize the dedication of the very limited surplus of materials and time free from the necessities of life to create the powerful form of musical expression called throat singing—which produces the effect of both voice and background instrument through the intense collaboration of two or more singers. Many hunter-gatherer societies had ample leisure time to develop their cultures of song and dance far more extensively than agricultural or industrial societies could.

Indeed music is the most accessible form of culture, since all that is required is people, time, and in some cases instruments. The power of African-based and Afro-Caribbean music—gospel, blues, jazz, reggae, ska, and hip hop—attests to how social groups with control of relatively little surplus but a very strong sense of social identity and cohesion can create powerful cultural change. Consider the brilliant transformation of empty steel shipping barrels in the Caribbean into steel drums, which today are not only percussion instruments but as steel "pans" also carry a melody. The evolution of hip hop into a highly diversified global mass culture in the late twentieth and early twenty-first centuries is a case study in cultural change fueled by new technology and the strengthening of youth cultures in Africa, Asia, and Latin America, which in the 1990s gained greater access to surplus to patronize culture.

THE QUANTITY OF SURPLUS CONTROLLED BY A SOCIAL GROUP AFFECTS THE EXTENT OF ITS CULTURE

Since aesthetic culture is a function of a social group's access to and control of surplus, and the actual production of works of art is dependent on how much of that surplus is directed toward patronage of the arts by those who control the surplus, the aesthetic culture produced by the group cannot be more extensive than what the patronage base makes possible. So the extent of the culture—the number of media involved, its longevity, its dissemination, its elaboration—depends on the group's access to and control of surplus material, time, or energy, and its ability to allocate some of this surplus in the form of patronage to artists or artisans.

Farming families in Western countries, for example, are a social group that in the nineteenth century controlled more surplus than they do today in the age of agribusiness. Agricultural fairs, even well into the twentieth century, were occasions to celebrate the culture of that social group. In the past fifty years, however, with their reduced access to and control of surplus, we see fewer agricultural fairs, and those that remain usually feature more urban culture in the form of midway rides, games, shows, and the material culture of the latest labor-saving machinery, rather than the traditional arts and crafts of agricultural society—such as country dancing and fiddling, judging crop and seed quality, animal training and domestication, and the crafts of food preparation and conservation, quilting, and sewing. County fairs always featured a share of city delights—that was part of the fun of the fair for farming families too—but what we can see in the shift from more rural to more urban content is that as the family farm declines in economic influence and farmers increasingly struggle just to stay on the land, farm families as a social group have less surplus to dispense on celebrating their own culture. The stronger urban culture moves in—so the county fair "ain't what it used to be."

This is not to say that social groups with greater access to and control of surplus have a better, richer, or finer culture, simply to note that it is likely to be more extensive. There will be more examples of it, it will be better known and more widely patronized than the culture of social groups with less access to or benefit from the surplus produced by that society. So it will be more influential, and considered more attractive by many both inside and outside that social group. To follow our example, this accounts for the appeal of urban culture to young people in rural areas the world over—even though the perceived benefits of that urban culture often prove to be beyond reach for those who migrate to the cities in order to participate in it.

Each Social Group Seeks Its Own Values in the Art It Patronizes

The great Russian filmmaker Vsevolod Pudovkin (1893–1953), during a discussion of the aesthetics of cinema in a socialist society in the 1920s or '30s, is said to have casually remarked: "After all, each social class seeks in its art the pathetic grandeur of its victory in its historic struggle."[1]

Of course Pudovkin was speaking of socioeconomic classes, but his remark can be applied to all social groups because they are all always involved in a process of struggle to sustain themselves and to grow stronger. The formation, growth, and dissolution of social groups is a constant process, in which each group is consciously or unconsciously struggling to at least maintain its position, and if possible to enhance it. In this struggle, its aesthetic culture is important, because it is the basis for identity and social cohesion, without which there is no social group.

"Victory" of a social group in this struggle to persist and gain greater control over its destiny may be recalled from the past, enjoyed in the present, or hoped for in the future. For example, after the British Civil Wars, during the interregnum of Lord Protector Oliver Cromwell (1599–1658) that began in 1653, English Royalists could only look back bitterly on their past position of power, while poet John Milton (1608–1674) celebrated the temporary victory of the Commonwealth and briefly served in Cromwell's cabinet; but with the Restoration after Cromwell's death in 1658, the Royalists regained their victorious position, and while Milton metaphorically lamented in his greatest poem, "Paradise Lost," first published in 1667,[2] other poets, dramatists, and composers were creating Restoration drama and music for the court of Charles II. When the "Glorious Revolution" of 1688 established a constitutional monarchy, midway between these two antithetical positions, the way was paved for a third group: the entrepreneurs and inventors who began the industrial revolution. Their culture's "victory" lay indefinitely in the future with only a modest beginning of manufacturing throughout the first half of the eighteenth century, but it had certainly arrived by the time of "the dark satanic mills" of the late eighteenth and early nineteenth centuries in the midlands and northern England.

Pudovkin's qualification of the concept of "grandeur" with "pathos" is significant. As a filmmaker in the postrevolutionary Soviet Union he had good reason to be aware of how hollow art can be when it is only about the grandeur of victory. Indeed we might categorize works that are only about "victory" as not being part of aesthetic culture at all, but moving into social-political culture as propaganda. The reference to pathos may also remind artists of the importance of "speaking truth to power"—especially when that power controls the artist's patronage. The Russian composer Dmitri Shostakovich (1906–1975), for example, wrestled with his relationships with state patronage throughout his career, as had the suprematist painter Kasimir Malevich (1879–1935) and the poet Vladimir Mayakovsky (1893–1930), who committed suicide in 1930, at the age of thirty-seven.

This struggle to avoid producing propaganda by evoking only the grandeur of a patronage group is by no means limited to Soviet artists. Consider the two contrasting examples by Jacques-Louis David (1748–1825), the artist most often associated with the French Revolution, whom we mentioned in chapter 5:

- David's powerful painting of the *Death of Marat* presents the *pathos* of the martyred leader, Jean-Paul Marat (1743–1793), murdered in the bathtub where he was trying to cure the skin disease he had contracted during his days of hiding in the sewers of Paris; but it also shows the pen and paper on which at the time of his death he was taking notes about opposition to the revolution in Normandy, whence his assassin Charlotte Corday (1768–1793) had journeyed from Caen—pointing to the *grandeur* of the great leader of the people, as David and some of his fellow Jacobins saw Marat, still working for the victory of the revolution, even at the moment of his death.
- By contrast, David's painting some years later of *Napoleon Crossing the Alps* shows Bonaparte rearing on his horse while the French army climbs the mountain behind him, a work of propaganda proclaiming only the *grandeur* of the imperial enterprise of bringing republicanism to Austria and central Europe—which is what David thought Napoleon's mission was.

Pathetic grandeur of a revolutionary: Jacques-Louis David (1748–1825), *Death of Marat*, 1793, oil on canvas, 165 x 128 cm (65 x 50⅜ in.), Musée Royal de Beaux-Arts, Brussels. Photo: © Royal Museums of Fine Arts of Belgium, Brussels; Grafisch Bureau Lefevre, Heule.

Grandeur without pathos: Jacques-Louis David (1748–1825), *Napoleon Crossing the St. Bernard Pass*, 1801/2, oil on canvas, 321 x 246 cm (126⅞ x 96⅞ in.), Châteaux de Versailles et de Trianon, Versailles. One of five versions painted by the artist due to widespread demand. Photo: Erich Lessing/Art Resource, NY.

As also noted in chapter 5, the other famous artist who responded to Napoleon's invasion was Ludwig van Beethoven, whose Third "Eroica" Symphony was initially dedicated to Napoleon's grandeur as a democrat and republican. But when Beethoven perceived Napoleon as an imperialist, he removed the dedication, so that the content of his great symphony might be recognized as the pathetic grandeur of the heroic struggle for democracy and independence. Beethoven had a clearer comprehension of Napoleon's mission than David.

So some works like David's *Napoleon* evoke only grandeur and degenerate into propaganda. On the other hand, if the work of art evokes *only* the pathos of the struggle of a social group, it may provide a moving document of a social problem, but it will not have the full complexity of a complete work of art. Like propaganda, a documentary record might be considered part of social-political rather than aesthetic culture. Documentary films and photography can be great works of art, as John Grierson (1898–1972) and

Another response to Napoleon's entry into Austria: Ludwig van Beethoven (1770–1827), Dedication page to the Third Symphony: *Eroica*, Opus 55, 1803, with Napoleon's name crossed out, Archiv der Gesellschaft der Musikfreunde, Vienna. Photo: Archiv der Gesellschaft der Musikfreunde in Wien.

others have proved, when they evoke the past, present, or potential grandeur as well as the pathos of the content they are documenting; but merely registering the pathos without that context results in an uninspiring record of human misery, as many well-intentioned socially conscious artists have found. Great photographs of poverty, such as the famous image of a woman and her children in the Depression by Dorothea Lange (1895–1965), stir us as complete works of art because in them—in the upraised head and the wearily watching eyes of the woman in this example—we can see the potential for grandeur that is denied by the pathos of her struggle in the face of the overwhelming social conditions around her.

Our seventeenth-century protagonists—Milton's poetry and Restoration drama and music—each evoked both the pathos and the grandeur of victory in the historic struggle of the social group whose culture they were contributing to. And the patronage available within each group responded positively to that pathetic grandeur when they saw it or heard it. Charles II and his court loved the Restoration poets and dramatists, as we may too. Because Milton was writing from within the Parlimentarian group that was ultimately linked to a much larger middle class who benefited from the English constitutional monarchy and subsequently from related democracies in the United States and the former British Empire long after Milton's death, his magnificent poetry eventually reached a much wider public and patronage from people in Britain and around the world.

In chapter 5 we noted the emergence of impressionism—a style that, although still representational, emphasized the formal qualities of light and color in scenes of everyday life. This cultural change was rejected by the old social-political order (remnants of the nobility and the industrial middle classes) that patronized the academies and the salons, but was embraced by the leading edge of the new group of capitalists whose profits derived from global investments. These new patrons, especially those in America, not only built personal collections but disseminated the new content of this new art by donating works to then new museums such as the Art Institute of Chicago or the Museum of Fine Arts in Boston—both Chicago and Boston being centers of new industrial capital in the 1880s and later.

Just a few weeks after the Stock Market Crash of 1929 that began the Great Depression, another new institution, the Museum of Modern Art, strongly supported by the Rockefeller family, opened in New York. In the following decade, in the midst of the Great Depression, still another new museum, the Museum of Non-Objective Art—now named after its founder, the Solomon R. Guggenheim Museum—was established in the same city.

Dorothea Lange (1895–1965), *Migrant Mother*, or *Destitute Pea Pickers in California: A 32-year-old mother of seven children. February 1936*. Nipomo, California, 1936, black-and-white photograph, Library of Congress, Washington, DC. Photo: Farm Security Administration, Office of War Information Photograph Collection, Prints and Photographs Division, Library of Congress, LC-USF34-9058-C.

Both of these Depression-era institutions were the product of patronage by the investment capital class. The financial sector based in Wall Street was strengthened by military-industrial investments throughout World War II and the Cold War, so it is not surprising that New York investors' patronage of the arts flourished, especially for new content—the powerful individualism of abstract expressionism was strongly supported in Manhattan's galleries and museums. Its values combined an appeal to the individual risk-taking of investors with their confidence in a visual language that is universally exchangeable, like their investments, not limited to the depiction of specific subject matter. Abstract expressionism quintessentially communicates both the pathos and the grandeur of the individual risk-taker in a universally exchangeable field of color, light, line, mass, and texture, through the sensuality of paint. So the dominant new patronage group of investment capitalists could recognize their pathetic grandeur—or more simply their values—in the new art. This recognition by patron groups of their underlying values in the content of the works produced by the artists they patronize gives us the critical third principle of cultural change:

Each social group seeks its own values in the art that it patronizes.

The most conscious members of any social group will respond with interest to new content evident in works of art that they can associate with their own values. Not all members of the group will be as perceptive, so many will continue to patronize works with previously acknowledged content. But once the leading members of the group begin to patronize art with the new content, sooner or later many members of the group will begin to recognize their values in the new art.

CULTURE CHANGES IN ACCORDANCE WITH CHANGES IN ACCESS TO SURPLUS

Changes in the access of a social group to surplus will have an impact on their capacity for patronage, and therefore on the art that they value. This process is made particularly vivid during and after revolutions—such as the American, the French, the Russian, or the Chinese revolutions—after which the ability of almost all social groups to access or control the surplus in their societies changed dramatically. The newly confident victors in the American Revolution patronized what we call federalist architecture, with its allusions to ancient Greek democracy and the Roman Republic, very different from the Georgian colonial buildings that preceded them. The French Revolution established the secular government as an important new patron, as the Louvre was opened to the public. The Russian collectors who had been patronizing Matisse and Picasso lost their fortunes, and the paintings they had purchased went into state museums, where they remain today. In 1949, the nationalist Chinese managed to move most of the last emperor's collection of Chinese art treasures out of mainland China to the island of Taiwan, where it is to be seen today (although still claimed by the People's Republic) in the National Palace Museum.

These sudden, dramatic changes are easy to observe. Yet gradual historical processes of cultural change are just as effective:

> *Changes in the degree of access to or control over surplus may arise from changes in a group's basic economy or changes in the group's social position; in either case they will result in changes in patronage.*

The discovery of oil, for example, beginning in the 1930s and extending its geographic reach gradually after World War II, transformed the material base of the Arabian Peninsula, especially along the shoreline of the Arabian Gulf. For several decades these formerly impoverished societies concentrated on the improvement of their basic infrastructure; today, however, the most conscious leaders in these societies—members of their royal families and others—are extending their patronage to build great museums, such as the Museum of Islamic Art in Qatar, and to develop the world's largest cultural district on Saadiyat Island off Abu Dhabi. The economic transformation due to oil has resulted in an equally dramatic cultural change.

The Great Depression of the 1930s steeply downgraded the social position of large numbers of North American farmers and working people. Their radically changed social position evoked *The Grapes of Wrath*, the novel by John Steinbeck (1902–1968) first published in 1939, and the even more popular film made of it in 1940. From within the ranks of this impoverished social group, songwriters extolled their pathetic grandeur in folk, blues, country, and bluegrass music, which the recording industry made available to them and others at relatively low prices. The economic recovery sparked by World War II, the prosperous 1950s, and the relatively affluent '60s then facilitated a surge in more affluent patronage for the music of this era and the production of still more forms of music by the singers and songwriters of the postwar period. So the farmers and working people's loss of control of surplus in the Depression resulted in a decrease in patronage for their former culture, but their altered conditions sparked the beginnings of a new culture for which they formed a significant part of the public, along with the greatly increased demographic of the "Baby Boom" in the 1960s and after.

QUANTITATIVE CHANGE IN PATRONAGE LEADS TO QUALITATIVE CULTURAL CHANGE

As described in chapter 6, the process of cultural change begins with the creative artist initiating new content in his or her work. The most conscious, leading members of the social group that identifies with and benefits from that new content will help make sure the artist or group of artists can continue to produce that content and continue to evolve their style, subjects, and media in support of that content. Because of the dynamic character of cultural change and the many ways it is communicated, more artists will become engaged with this new content, and patronage may expand to support the growing body of new content.

Conversely, the declining patronage capability of a social group with decreasing access to surplus will result in fewer works of art being produced with content that relates to the "pathetic grandeur" of that social group. Fewer artists will be attracted to produce works of that kind, and the subject matter or style that may be associated with that content may fade into cultural history.

A particularly clear example of this principle at work is afforded by the history of the Group of Seven, artists who developed a national school of landscape painting in Canada in the second and third decade of the twentieth century. The Canadian landscape had formerly been painted according to nineteenth-century European conventions that generally ignored the specific character of the rugged land of lakes and rocks that geologists call the Laurentian Shield. Influenced by the daring of the Fauve painters of France, where some of them had studied, and by the example of some Scandinavian painters who were also exploring the unique qualities of the north in similar landscapes, this new group of Canadian artists around the beginning of the second decade of the twentieth century started sketching *en plein air*, recording the vivid colors and powerful shapes of the northern landscape they knew. Their earliest attempts were exhibited just before World War I, and they continued to produce outstanding paintings with this new content before, during, and after the World War I years. Throughout the war and for some years after it, British economic investment in Canada was curtailed due to the enormous cost of the conflict in Europe, so that Canadian nationalist interests were able to grow stronger, especially in mining stocks. As would be expected according to these dynamic principles of cultural change, a few of the most conscious members of this nationalist group, along with doctors and other professionals who held similar patriotic ideas, began to use their greater capacity for patronage to encourage and purchase the works of these artists. By 1921, despite the untimely death in 1917 of Tom Thomson (1877–1917), the greatest artist among them, these painters were able to hold the first of a series of exhibitions of major works of art that consciously proclaimed their new national landscape content. Of course there were critics and patrons who resisted their rise to prominence, but as the decade of the 1920s rolled on they became the dominant force in visual art, at least in Anglophone Canada.

After World War I, British economic investment was never again able to dominate the Canadian economy as it formerly had; by 1926 U.S. investment had supplanted it as the leading factor in Canadian economic life. As a result, the Canadian nationalist patronage group was unable to hold the position of relative prominence it had briefly enjoyed. After 1929 the Great Depression reduced the patronage they had been able to provide to a meager level. In 1933, the Group of Seven officially disbanded into a larger "Canadian Group of Painters." It comprised many of the followers, those artists who had responded to the increased patronage for the new content and were able to follow the new style that had accompanied it almost as a formula: rocky foreground, lake in the middle ground and far shore at a high horizon, often with pine trees bending in the wind. It is noteworthy that although several of the group continued to paint well after this date, an exhibition of major works in the Canadian landscape style would include relatively few paintings later than 1926, the year when its patrons began to lose their competitive advantage. The one exception, Lawren Harris (1885–1970), was independently wealthy from a family fortune in agricultural implement production, and so was able to continue painting major canvases, extending his range to increasingly formal studies of Arctic and Rocky Mountains subjects, eventually joining a Transcendentalist group of abstract artists.

Thus the quantitative rise and then relative decline of the power and wealth of the nationalist patronage group can be seen to result first in the growth, spread, and influence of the Canadian national landscape content, style, and subject matter, then in its relative decline as the "Canadian Group" followers supplanted the original initiating artists who had achieved this powerful cultural change. Of course there are many heroic individual accomplishments in this "historic struggle," as well as much pathos in their life stories, among both the patrons and the artists. Understanding the general phenomenon does not in any way reduce, but rather enhances, our appreciation of the power of the works of art in themselves, as they reveal the splendor of the northern Canadian landscape. But the lesson for students of cultural change is clear:

> *Quantitative change in patronage results in qualitative change of the works of art.*

By qualitative change we do not necessarily mean "better" works of art. Increased patronage can result in the proliferation of mediocrity, as in the glut of operas produced for the opera houses of mid-seventeenth-century Venice, or as in B-movies from Hollywood to Bollywood. The point of this principle is simply that the source of any qualitative change in aesthetic culture, for better or worse, can be found in the quantitative build-up or decrease of the patronage available to the producers of that change.

Cultural Validation and Invalidation by Dominant Cultures Affects All Others

Because values and cultural meanings are fundamental to the cohesion and stability of the group, social groups strive to ensure that their values are embedded in the art they patronize. When a social group, country, or social class controls so much surplus that it becomes dominant—a ruling class or an imperial power—it often seeks to enhance its dominance by cultural means. Some empires actually validate the cultures of the conquered as the best way of increasing their own position: the rulers of the Ottoman Empire, for example, invited the greatest artists and artisans from the conquered peoples to settle in their capital and work for them. The Roman Empire took over much of ancient Greek culture. The Mongols savagely destroyed entire cities that they conquered in central and west Asia, yet a generation or two later in many places the Mongol warriors had converted to Islam, and the Muslim cultures of those regions reasserted themselves. For most empires or dominant groups, however, the strategy is to *invalidate* the culture of the conquered or dominated social groups so that they adopt the "superior" culture of the imperial center. This too is cultural change!

> *Dominant social groups not only assert the priority of the culture they patronize, but also seek to invalidate the culture of other groups.*

In slave-owning societies, owners have almost exclusive access to and control of surplus, and use it not only to patronize their own culture, but also to ensure that the slaves (and usually other social orders as well) accept their culture as the primary—or only—criterion of value. Although it is important not to overemphasize slavery in ancient Egypt, since it was only one aspect of a complex social structure, that culture does provide the most striking instance of this principle of domination, as the works of art and architecture that characterize its burial culture were intended to convince everyone that absolute control of their lives by the pharaohs and their priests extended even beyond their rulers' deaths. Domination by the slave-owners' cultural values in the antebellum southern United States was not nearly as absolute, but clearly prescribed the terms in which African-American slaves could utilize their very meager surplus of time, energy, and materials in their religious and musical culture; heroically, African-American culture planted the roots of gospel, blues, and jazz music under these conditions.

This principle of cultural change is equally evident in feudal societies, where the landholding nobles' culture is recognized as "high art," whereas that of the peasants is seen as "low" or "folk" art. Only after the feudal lords have lost their power do subsequent social groups begin to prize the peasants' folk art, often as a root culture of the nation-states that supplanted the feudal regimes. India's caste society was the most extreme, communicating absolute disdain for "untouchables" and establishing a clear hierarchy of cultural valuation among all other levels of society. Princes and brahmins were at the top, the *kshatriya* warrior culture secondary, and the cultures of merchants and peasants considered at steeply lower levels.

Language is a direct imprint of the cultural influence of one group on another. The Romans left behind Latin roots in the languages of much of their Empire, from Romania to Portugal. After the Normans conquered England in 1066, their dominance not only convinced the Anglo-Saxons to adopt many French words into their language, but also persuaded them that their own short (mostly four-letter) words for intimate body parts and functions were somehow "dirty." Anglophone children learning to speak are still punished for using the Anglo-Saxon words, and almost a thousand years later they are still not admissible in "polite" society. Cultural domination casts a long shadow.

Throughout Europe, court culture asserted its superiority over "low culture" forms until royalty definitively lost its dominant patronage position with respect to the industrial middle class in the nineteenth century. In Germany for example, a "middle" level of culture known as *Biedermeier* emerged at that time. Much earlier, and more profoundly, by the seventeenth century the bourgeois material and social-political culture of individual enterprise already resulted in rising patronage for dramas like those of Shakespeare and Molière, and portraits like those of Rembrandt and Frans Hals (1580–1666), all of which still speak to us so powerfully of the grandeur and pathos of individual character. Meanwhile, the aristocrats of most western European nations continued with their patronage first of baroque and later of rococo art forms, contrasting their genteel life with that of the merchants, manufacturers, and peasants; but by the end of the eighteenth century, signaled clearly by the French Revolution of 1789 to 1793 and the subsequent revolutions in France in 1830 and 1848, the bourgeoisie were increasingly able to set the agenda and the standards for intercultural valuation.

When a dominant social group establishes its culture over conquered societies, it is usually a very harsh process. In the late nineteenth century, the Canadian government in colonizing the Pacific coast (today's British Columbia) outlawed the potlatch ceremonies of the First Nations peoples, who had developed a highly elaborate sculptural, dance, dramatic, and musical culture based on ceremonies of gift giving. With the help of the church, which perceived unhealthy pagan religious significance in these ceremonies in which the magnificent cultural artifacts of these civilizations were redistributed among leading families of neighboring and intermarrying clans, the government not only outlawed the potlatch, but also seized the artifacts and sold them or deposited them in museums. It was not until the late twentieth century, when the aboriginal peoples had regained their strength, were making claims for return of their lands, and had educated some of their own sons and daughters as lawyers and curators, that this theft of these culturally invaluable objects was recognized for what it was. Even then, it was only in a few limited instances where the government was able to identify objects that had been impounded from specific groups, and where museums able to preserve them had been provided with government subsidy, that objects were repatriated. This particular struggle against cultural domination continues.

Aboriginal peoples throughout North and South America, Australia, and elsewhere have suffered over more than five centuries as Spanish, Portuguese, Dutch, French, English, and American settlers systematically undertook to eliminate or at least completely devalue the indigenous cultures of the lands they occupied. This was often done in the name of "progress" or "assimilation," as the children of indigenous people were forcibly taken to residential schools distant from their homes and families, where they were punished even for speaking to each other in their own language, keeping their own names, or manifesting any signs of their own culture.

Barry encountered one of the most vivid examples of this practice in a museum in northern Canada some years ago. A display case in the museum held an outstanding sequence of beaded moccasins in the style of a local band. Each pair of moccasins was larger than the one beside it, and all were in pristine, "mint" condition. When I inquired as to how these beautiful examples of craftsmanship had been acquired in all sizes and in such fine condition, I learned that a woman whose mother had given them to her as a child had deposited them in the museum many years later. Not being able to prevent her little daughter's departure for the government-mandated residential school at a very young age, her mother had made for her when she first left a fine pair of moccasins to fit her tiny feet. But of course the residential school told the child immediately after she arrived that she must wear shoes, and that these signs of her own culture would not be tolerated. So she had put them away unworn. But when she returned home the next summer, she could not bring herself to tell her mother that she was not allowed to wear them, so each year she carried another pair to the school, hid them away, and thus preserved the entire magnificent sequence in perfect condition for the museum. Today, Canada's aboriginal people have fought for and won partial redress for the abuses of the residential schools. However, they are still in the process of learning how thoroughgoing this abuse has been affecting generations of their people, their social organization, and family lives. The rediscovery, revival, and validation of their own culture is a most important survival tool, which is possible as aboriginal peoples strive to gain more legal, political, and financial control over their land and institutions.

Many artists in oppressed groups have found both direct and indirect ways to resist the devaluation of their cultures by ruling groups. When the Duke of Alba viciously attacked the cities and towns of the Low Countries to enforce obedience to Spain's ruling Counter-Reformation religious culture, Pieter Brueghel the Elder (1525–1569)—who painted many commissions for the ruling Spaniards and their Flemish agents—depicted genre scenes that showed the people of the Netherlands celebrating their own "folk" festivals. His most memorable painting, *The Slaughter of the Innocents*, is a vivid metaphor for the Spanish army's horrendous aggressions against Flemish towns and villages. Poet and playwright Johann Wolfgang von Goethe (1749–1842) may actually have admired Bonaparte, but the spirited content of his work nevertheless led Germans' cultural resistance to the dominance of French culture imposed by Napoleon. Writers, artists, and musicians in

India reasserted the values of Indian civilization against the British *raj*. The Filipino author José Rizal (1861–1896) in 1887 and 1891 published two great novels that satirized the Spanish ruling class and assured his fellow citizens that their own lifestyle and culture were of value, against the overwhelming presence of the last days of the Spanish Empire; the poem known as "*Ultimo Adios*," which he wrote in prison while awaiting his execution by the Spanish Army, still lives today as an expression of Filipinos' love for their country.

Sometimes reestablishing respect for a dominated and downgraded culture is simply a question of reviving traditional art forms, but in many instances an artist or a group of artists lead the way by reasserting the value in the people and places around him or her, thereby refuting the notion spread by the dominant group that anything of real value comes from them. During the Indian struggle for independence, Mahatma Gandhi wittily denied any claim of British cultural superiority when he was asked what he thought of Western civilization and answered, "I think it would be a very good idea."

Oppression of women by men has been and continues to be the most widespread and persistent form of domination in the world. Until recently even in developed Western countries, most women did not control their own wealth (when they had it) and therefore could not be patrons. The idea that women were incapable of producing truly significant art and that they were intellectually not equal to men was the dominant ideology of male culture (both East and West) well into the twentieth century, and still persists in too many places. Today well over half of the women and girls in the world continue to suffer from this material, physical, sociopolitical, and cultural oppression by men. Worse still, many of the men who oppress women, guided by their (male) religious leaders, are willing to fight to the death to preserve their right to do so. Fear of women's equality fuels our sharpest conflicts.

There have been and continue to be many women's movements fighting against this oppression—particularly during the battles for decolonization following World War II. There is reason to believe that the cultural consciousness of women will grow exponentially in the coming decades, leading to their greater control over their own lives and culture. There are certainly more women in more countries controlling more wealth than ever before. In the United States as of 2009, 43 percent of the top tier financial group is female. This is leading to increased support for women's education, health, and cultural expression both in the United States and in countries in the developing world (where the ruling classes doubtless see in this trend American cultural imperialism). More women than ever before have risen to the ranks of professor, dean, chancellor, and president of top universities, encouraging historians in each of the arts to "discover" the previously undervalued contribution of significant women in all art forms. In addition to being recognized as artists, women today are increasingly active as patrons in their own right.

By devaluing the other group's culture, a dominant social group makes it exceedingly difficult for an oppressed group to develop or sustain its own forms of patronage, thereby weakening the less dominant group's culture all the more. Nevertheless the oppressed group's culture remains latent, and may rise to conscious articulation, and even find patronage, at moments of intense struggle. The Harlem Renaissance of African-American artists, musicians, and writers in the 1920s and 1930s is one example of such a cultural breakthrough by a community whose culture had long been repressed. Despite their initial difficulty in finding patronage, the artists who participated in that movement for cultural change are now celebrated as the precursors of the vital African-American visual and performing art, music, and literature of today.

In the past few centuries, a new method of dominance of one social group over another has appeared with the rise of the cultural industries of mass culture. Mass culture refers to cultural forms and expressions that enjoy widespread popularity. Not all of it is characterized by cultural domination: a lot of mass culture is produced as a result of the creativity of artists supported by the slender patronage of social groups that are not competing for social or political dominance. Nevertheless, in the main, mass culture has become one of the most effective means that dominant social groups have to communicate their cultural values broadly, and to influence masses of people over the long term.

Religion was initially the most powerful means of communicating the cultural values of the ruling classes in most ancient and feudal societies, especially those based on the energy of slaves or serfs. Pharaohs, sultans, kings, and nobles almost always worked closely with priests, monks, or imams to ensure that all other social groups not only accepted but literally worshipped the spiritual as well as the aesthetic values of the dominant culture. Religious institutions were therefore fundamentally conservative, and any changes in the values they taught were likely to reflect the rise of a new social group challenging the dominant status quo—most clearly exemplified by the rise of Protestantism in sixteenth-century Europe, which, as sociologist Max Weber (1864–1920) famously observed, championed the values of the rising mercantile capitalist class in northern Europe at that time. Educational institutions, originally under the control of the church, also provided—as they still do—a major means of transmission of cultural values to all social groups, especially after public education of children was made compulsory.

The development of the technology to reproduce multiple copies of words and images—printing and printmaking—provided the dominant social group with a new means of communicating its cultural values not through religious or educational institutions alone, but through the dissemination of the products of cultural industries. In Korea and China, where printing was first discovered, the earliest prints are of religious (Buddhist) subjects, or illustrate myths and fables extolling virtues or warning against vices. Similar content was produced after Johannes Gutenberg (c. 1400–1468) began printing with movable type in Europe in 1440. Subsequent technological developments have made possible mass cultural industries that disseminate almost every discipline of the arts to a broad audience—motion pictures, sound recordings, radio, television, and today's electronic media. Dominant social groups impart their content to these media through their control of networks, distribution channels, and the organizations that produce the content in recording studios, sound stages, or editing labs. The continued development of new media further intensifies the effect of these cultural industries; as Marshall McLuhan observed, the previous medium usually becomes the content of the new technology.

This extension of the principle of cultural domination via mass cultural industries has directly affected what might otherwise be considered the rise of a new patronage group over the past century and a half—the organization and growth of trade unions. Since to some extent and in some places unions have achieved greater leisure time and social security for their members by winning rights to holidays, health benefits, and pensions, it might be expected that the workers and their families who have benefited from these hard-won victories in physical culture might utilize their slightly enhanced capacity for patronage of new content in works of art. To a limited extent this has been true, from union songs and the labor press to patronage for the architecture of social housing projects in Vienna and elsewhere in Europe around the turn of the twentieth century. But for the most part the dominance of mass culture provided by the cultural industries has determined the character of the limited access of the organized working class in capitalist countries to cultural expression, and in many cases has conditioned them to validate mass culture over any alternative content.

The 1950s and 1960s witnessed the height of cultural dominance of these cultural industries by the United States. Locked in a "cold war" with the Soviet Union to control hearts and minds as well as countries and economies, it was critically important for the United States to control the creation and dissemination of mass culture. Looking back, we can see how the content of American television at that time reinforced the values of the dominant culture: TV was almost exclusively white, predominantly male, and insistently "middle class." A typical example was the hit television series called *Father Knows Best*, on network TV from 1954 to 1960. That was a big cultural change from the socially conscious mass culture of the mid-1940s (in films and on radio), when the United States and the Soviet Union were allies in the fight against fascism. Making that sudden cultural change from the 1940s to the 1950s required more than the "velvet glove" of mass culture; the "iron fist" was the series of House UnAmerican Activities Committee hearings of 1953, a witch-hunt led by Senator Joseph McCarthy (1908–1957) to persecute and remove from any position of influence hundreds of professors, government employees, and artists for being "communist sympathizers." Ten leading Hollywood writers were blacklisted and were unable to work for decades, even after McCarthy had been discredited, because their work had been so devalued by the dominant culture. Hundreds of others lost their creative livelihoods, in many instances forced to withdraw from cultural work.

It would seem to be somewhat more difficult today for dominant groups to manipulate mass culture. Changes in technology that give people access to tools of creation and dissemination of culture, critical awareness of media, higher education levels among a greater proportion of the population, and the growth of the knowledge economy are greatly reducing the influence of dominant cultures and dominant social groups. Social networking programs on the Internet provide far more opportunity for creative participation by artists, audience, and patrons, in contrast to the relative omnipotence formerly enjoyed by TV networks, record companies, and Hollywood film studios. Nevertheless, the fundamental role of mass culture as an agent of cultural domination persists, and daily grows more sophisticated in finding ways to reassert control. The themes of *Father Knows Best* have been successively reprised in the past fifty years with more sardonic humor—but ultimately with comparable effect—by characters like Archie Bunker or the Simpsons. "Entertainment is betrayal," philosopher Theodor Adorno (1903–1969) observed, referring to the ways in which the interests of the mass audience are betrayed by the cultural industries that entertain them by enforcing social control; fortunately for him, Adorno did not live to see "reality TV."

INTERCULTURAL ASPECTS OF CULTURAL
CHANGE OFFER NEW OPPORTUNITIES

Thus far we have analyzed how the interaction of artist and patronage results in cultural change within one social group. But of course most societies are a complex mix of many groups with different identities, ethnic backgrounds, and cultures. Social groups from many regions and countries interact in other ways as well, such as trade, travel, and war. Cultural interaction among artists and patrons of different social groups leads to new subjects, new styles, and new content.

The growth of "world music" through festivals, recording, and mass distribution of performances from around the world starting in the late 1980s is an enormous cultural change. Prior to this time, music created by "ethnic groups" or "cultural minorities" (many of whom were actually former majorities who had been conquered and dispersed) was considered to be subject matter for ethnologists studying dying cultures. The successful struggles for decolonization that reached a peak in the 1970s (by which time there were very few political colonies left on earth) and the social and political changes in developed countries, especially among young people, who had the financial means to travel and the educational attainment to appreciate other cultures, broke down barriers established by hundreds of years of colonization and created a movement called "world music," in which all musical forms are equal, whatever the economic or political status of the culture of origin. Artists and musicians from countries along the historic Silk Road, from African countries, and from Latin America could now earn money from performances and from recording, leading to the encouragement of more artists, new musical forms, and continuous cultural change. Quantitative increase in patronage was producing a qualitative change in the music.

Current developments in information technology, availability of cheap transportation, and the increasing migrations of people looking for greater economic, political, and cultural opportunities facilitate even more intercultural contact and collaboration. However it needs to be said that these are merely the tools of intercultural collaboration. Without the attitude that intercultural collaboration is a positive constructive force, these same tools can be used (and are in some societies) to invalidate or devalue other cultures—to create and enforce a hierarchy of aesthetic cultures, with the culture of the dominant social group on top.

Intercultural aspects of cultural change can be seen as developing in three phases: multiculturalism, interculturalism, and intraculturalism:

- *Multiculturalism* was pioneered by Canada, already a bilingual country, but also one that depended and continues to depend on immigration as a source of labor and wealth. Starting in the 1960s, Canada's federal government introduced a policy of multiculturalism that validated the languages and cultures of immigrant groups—in contrast to the United States at that time, which prided itself on being a "melting pot," the Canadian metaphor was of a cultural mosaic. Because Canadian culture was itself so dominated by U.S. culture and therefore devalued, the possibility that the more northern country could ever become a homogeneous "melting pot" did not in any case really exist. National, provincial, and local governments provided and continue to provide funding for heritage language classes and the preservation of ethnic cultural forms. Yet this multicultural approach has distinct limitations, resulting in a kind of "side-by-side play," in which ethnic culture is accepted but is not valorized as "serious," and therefore does not benefit from patronage outside government or the specific cultural group itself.[3]
- *Interculturalism*, by which is meant collaboration among different cultures, is more characteristic of the situation today. Interculturalism arises from the interdependence in an international world of many different societies and their cultures. Most developed countries have become dependent on immigrant labor and on the cheap products imported from many of the same countries that are also exporting labor. Social groups, whether living in close proximity or working together at a distance across time zones, are interdependent as never before and need to understand each other's cultures in order to function. Operators in call centers in India need to understand the culture of the callers in order to help them trouble-shoot computer problems. The growing social-political human rights culture has opened up immigration to intellectuals and artists from many countries. Training students to be effective workers, managers, and leaders in a globalized world means providing the educational tools for them to understand and experience other cultures and alternative perspectives. This has led to teaching positions in universities and colleges for a greater diversity of professors with different points of view. At first these approaches—postcolonial studies, aboriginal studies, women's studies, gay and gender studies, and African-American studies—were tentative, not at all valued by the dominant culture and under threat of cancellation. Women's history courses, to pick one example, were often said to be subjects for women who

couldn't learn much else. The growth of patronage by the specific cultural groups themselves—both students enrolling in courses and successful alumni funding them—has played a decisive role in changing the face of education from unicultural to intercultural in two generations. Many museums and art galleries are becoming less unicultural in their approach to modern and contemporary art. In the past generation, a growing number have begun to collect contemporary art from Asia, Africa, India, and Latin America—regions that formerly had not been considered significant for their contemporary culture by many of the dominant cultures of the West. The tradition of displaying historical art by "school" or country is increasingly being replaced by thematic installations that allow for intercultural considerations and the dynamic of cultural change.

- *Intraculturalism*: If the interdependence of social groups and their cultures is a motivating force for intercultural change, then we might understand intracultural change as part of the great challenge and opportunity of a global existence. Intracultural change is further explored in chapter 9.

CONCLUSION: SEVEN INTERRELATED PRINCIPLES

The seven principles of cultural change have been presented under separate headings as the seven sections of this chapter. However, they clearly constitute a coordinated and consequent sequence of principles that, taken together, explain why and how cultures change:

- Each Social Group Has Its Own Culture
- The Quantity of Surplus Controlled by a Social Group Impacts the Extent of Its Culture
- Each Social Group Seeks Its Own Values in the Art It Patronizes
- Culture Changes in Accordance with Changes in Access to Surplus
- Quantitative Change in Patronage Leads to Qualitative Cultural Change
- Cultural Validation and Invalidation by Dominant Cultures Affects All Others
- Intercultural Aspects of Cultural Change Offer New Opportunities

We have previously made the point that the four kinds of culture are closely interrelated, constantly affecting each other. Now we see also that these seven principles are equally interrelated, one giving rise to or annulling the effects of another. Understanding any specific cultural change requires a careful analysis of how these principles are at work and how they are affecting one another, as well as the interplay among the four types of culture that provides a specific context for their operation.

Our concluding two chapters show how these principles can help us to comprehend better the world around us. In chapter 8 we look at how the principles apply to changes in the environment and our consciousness of it, while in chapter 9 we explore how they can be applied to help us understand and participate in cultural change today.

NOTES

1. Pudovkin may have been referring to the writings of Georgii Plekhanov (1857–1918), author of *Art and Society* (1912–1913), the standard text on culture in early Soviet Russia.

2. Milton's earliest notes for the poem may date from 1639 to 1640, but his letters contemporary with its completion and publication express his profound sense of loss and betrayal after the Restoration.

3. Inuit and Northwest Coast art are an exception, as their carvings and prints have attracted mainstream cultural institutions and many private patrons.

CHAPTER 8

Cultural Change and the Environment

THE Durance River splashes down its valley from high in the Alpes Maritimes of northern Provence, past the town of Embrun. That is where Barry went with our Lordculture team from Paris in the summer of 2005, to help a group known as the *radeliers* plan a visitor center that would document and interpret the proud history of the raftsmen who had once been vital to the French Empire and its navy, bringing down from the mountain slopes the felled timber that would become masts and spars in the age of wooden ships. Nowadays Embrun is a quiet town of slight interest to skiers and cultural tourists, offering splendid views of the surrounding mountains and the picturesque valley from the higher slopes around it; but from the late Middle Ages through to the mid-nineteenth century, it was part of an industry vital to the commerce, defense, and imperial exploits of France—a center of French material and social-political culture.

Today we see the Durance valley as a potentially idyllic refuge from the pollution that threatens so many other waterways and their environs. In fact, it is threatened by many of the same factors of environmental degradation that concern us around the world. Our heightened consciousness of the environment and what our material, physical, and social-political culture has done and is doing to it inevitably has a significant effect on our aesthetic culture as well.

In the early 1980s, Gail and Barry were irritated when we took our children to a beach or other natural attraction and were told by the kids that the water or the soil was polluted. Unfortunately, the kids were right and we were wrong to be annoyed. The awakening of an environmental consciousness, first signaled by the publication by Houghton Mifflin of Rachel Carson's *Silent Spring* in 1962, is one of the major cultural changes of the past half-century. Here again aesthetic culture is not a passive reflector, but an active participant, as artists of all kinds have played and are playing a major role in raising environmental consciousness, through their works and through their lives. In the visual arts there is even a specific category of subject matter and content called "environmental art."

We began this book by asking "Why does culture change?" This chapter applies the analysis and principles that we have developed to ask: "Why has our culture developed this consciousness of the environment? And how has our consciousness of the environment changed our culture?"

The short answer is suggested by the principle of quantitative buildup or depletion leading to qualitative change that we identified in the preceding chapter. The depletion of fish stocks in the ocean, for example, has made us aware that overfishing by the big trawlers must stop; so the political culture of some countries has established quotas for cod and other species. The buildup of CO_2 in the atmosphere has effected a qualitative change in the design of automobiles and a decision by some people to use bicycles or public transit. The Kyoto Accords of 1997 and subsequent agreements may be seen as an attempt to translate quantitative change into qualitative differences in the way we live.

A more substantive answer—one that is more relevant to how aesthetic culture is involved—needs to begin by tracing the root of our environmental awareness to the transformation of nature that we have identified as the defining characteristic of human culture. To meet our basic needs in material and physical culture we transform nature for food, water, clothing, and shelter; but there is a fifth basic need that we meet through the transformation of nature—the need for energy. Every society—every social group—needs energy. Of all the resources of a society, a source of energy is the most fundamental, because energy is needed for every other activity. Once water, food, and shelter are secured, a source of energy is required in order for the society to maintain itself, let alone to advance. Surplus energy is therefore an extremely valuable resource.

Further, the importance of a source of energy is obvious to all members of the society, whether they are chiefs or villagers, pharaohs or slaves, kings or commoners, prime ministers or citizens. Access to and control of surplus energy is one of the most important surpluses that a dominant social group can achieve, and one that all other social groups must be aware of. Hence an awareness of how energy is produced and distributed is a crucial question for the social and environmental consciousness of all groups in any society. A group that controls a surplus of energy is in a strong position not only to patronize works of art that reflect its values, but also to assert those values as authoritative to other social groups and to communicate those values in whatever form of mass culture is available in that historical period (illustrating another of the principles we identified in the foregoing chapter).

Transformation of the environment to provide the energy we need—especially the surplus energy that makes a vital difference to the lives and fortunes of any social group—fundamentally affects the values we hold dear, the values that are expressed in our aesthetic culture:

> *Awareness of the sources of energy, and the struggle of social groups for access to and control of those sources, has a profound effect on the values that any society, or any social group, patronize in their aesthetic culture.*

Sources of energy may remain static for long periods of time, but when a new source is discovered or developed, it is additive—that is, the previous sources of energy and the environmental and other values or meanings associated with them are retained, possibly for a very long time, while the new source and the values associated with it are added to the mix. But because creative artists and leading patrons respond to what's new in their world, it is the new values associated with the new source of energy that are most distinctive for the aesthetic culture of each period.

All four kinds of culture are directly affected by changes in the source of energy, itself a factor in material culture. In Mesoamerican cultures, for example, where the main source of energy was correctly understood as being the sun, sacrificial rituals and even the famous ball game played with a rubber ball on a stone court combined aspects of physical, social-political, and aesthetic culture, often with symbolic references to the sun. Thus, especially in regard to the values associated with a society's energy sources, aesthetic culture responds to changes in the other three types—material, physical, and social-political culture—through the medium of patronage by the social group most in control of the energy source. Changing attitudes to the environment will be expressed in both social-political and aesthetic culture—but in addition the patronage of the dominant social group will be influenced by their perception of where value arises in relation to the source of energy and how they appropriate their environment in order to control and distribute surplus energy from it. Many of these perceptions of meaning and value related to the way in which energy is derived from the environment may range far afield from what is usually considered as "environmental" consciousness—yet they are all rooted in an awareness of the importance of energy and who controls it. The German word *zeitgeist*—the spirit of the times—is often used even in English to express such a complex of additive, iterative, and self-reinforcing values.

The earliest source of energy, one that has remained essential to the very concept of what it means to be human, is cooperative labor. The very name of "hunting and gathering" societies tells us that the source of energy for the earliest groups of *Homo sapiens* was the cooperative labor of the men and women in a hunting and gathering band. Gathering required the wisdom taught by earlier generations of which plants to collect and use, which to ignore; the leaves or fruit of some plants are poisonous if eaten raw and could be safely consumed only after being prepared in ways that had to be carefully taught to each generation. In many early societies, gathering probably provided the staple diet, so that hunting depended on the amount of surplus energy—cooperative labor—that could be devoted to it. *Homo sapiens* is a relatively weak, slow individual compared to most predators. Much of our earliest meat diet probably came from scavenging, because in order to hunt effectively at all early humans had to learn to cooperate, not only in the actual hunt but also in the making of hunting weapons such as spears, *atlatls*, and eventually bows and arrows. The production of projectile points by chipping stone stimulated a division of labor, so that those who were most proficient at this highly skilled task might devote more time to it. They would have to be supported—patronized—by the hunters, who had to learn to work together to bring down beasts that were in many cases larger and faster than they were.

It is therefore not surprising that depictions of animals—the targets of hunters—are the subject matter of some of the earliest examples of aesthetic culture. But it is also noteworthy that much of the culture of hunter-gatherer groups—including the few extant today—expresses the *identity* of the group, on masks, shields, carved figures, or totems. To maintain a hunting economy that was possible only to the extent that surplus cooperative labor was available required a strong sense of group identity among the toolmakers, projectile point makers, and the actual hunting party:

Cultural expressions of group identity were—and still are—affirmations of a belief in the surplus energy value of the cooperative labor of that group.

Much has been written about the heightened environmental consciousness of hunter-gatherers, their feeling of kinship with the land. This is true to the extent that far less technology is involved in the interface with nature, and there is generally no social-political culture of individual land ownership to alienate band members from their hunting territory. On the other hand, the band's claim on that territory is essential to its survival, and any threats to their sovereignty must be met with determined resistance. Here again we can see how the expression of identity in the band's members' aesthetic culture, inscribed on weapons of defense if necessary, is rooted in their environmental consciousness and their awareness that their source of surplus energy derives from their ability to work and hunt together. Nevertheless, it is important to note that:

> *Hunting and gathering culture necessarily respected the habitat of the plants and animals on which it depended.*

Domestication of animals added a new source of energy over thousands of years. Two relatively recent examples provide striking instances of the cultural changes resulting from the introduction of a new source of surplus energy from this source:

- Introduction of the Saharan and North African camel saddle, probably around the fourth or fifth centuries of the Common Era, transformed the material culture of the Bedouin, Tuareg, and other peoples of those lands, as long-distance travel became possible not only for trade, but also for exploration, as the famous journey of Ibn Battuta in the fourteenth century attests. The *Hajj*, the pilgrimage to Mecca that all Muslims are enjoined to undertake at least once in a lifetime, could become a central feature of Muslim life throughout their desert lands, thanks to the camel. Camel racing and the decoration of camel gear are just some of the resulting characteristics of these cultures.
- The Spanish Conquistadors' introduction of the domesticated horse onto the plains of western North America in the sixteenth and seventeenth centuries revolutionized the hunter-gatherer and incipient agricultural indigenous peoples of those prairie lands. A glance at a buffalo skin or robe painted to illustrate a chief's or a whole tribe's achievements in stealing horses from neighboring groups shows how directly the awareness of the importance of this new source of surplus energy was grasped by the artists of the Sioux, Cheyenne, Blackfoot, and others, and supported by the patronage of the chiefs, the band councils, or the families that owned them.

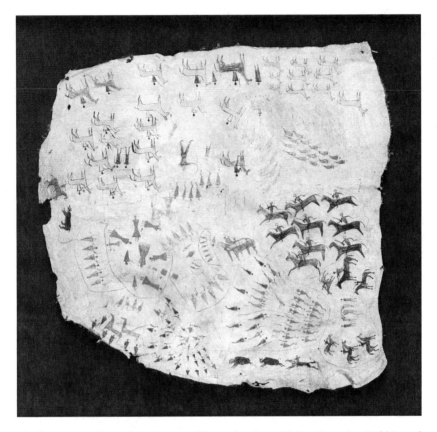

The horse transformed indigenous life on the Great Plains: Running Rabbit and White Man (son of Running Rabbit?), Siksika (Blackfoot) Nation, Alberta, Canada, war exploit robe, 1909, pigment on buffalo skin, 190 x 170 cm (74⅞ x 67 in.), Royal Ontario Museum, Edmund Morris Collection (977 x 1.3), Toronto. Photo: © ROM, used with permission.

As we have already observed, adopting the values associated with a new source of energy does not annul the values associated with the previous source: the process is cumulative. Thus, cooperative labor and the consequent need to assert the identity of a cooperative group remain important to pastoral and agricultural peoples as well. The assertion of identity may be immediately recognizable in the garments worn by a group, especially among itinerant pastoral people who need to recognize each other as they follow their herds from one pasture to another. In India, for instance, the

Rabari sheep, camel, and goat herders of the arid lands of western Rajasthan and eastern Gujarat traditionally wore distinctive turbans, while Rabari women appeared in cotton prints that allowed informed observers to know not only what area they came from, but also their marital status. Thus they could enter into Rajput market centers like Balotra and be distinguished from the other groups in town—such as the Maali market gardeners or the village genealogists and story tellers, the Bhaats, each of whom had their own distinctive patterns printed on cloth. As the way of life of all of these peoples has changed over the past fifty years, so the need to express their identity in this attractive, portable way has declined, and the best place to see their beautiful printed patterns today is in the Anokhi Museum of Hand Printing in Amber, near Jaipur, the capital of Rajasthan.

Animal rights activists today point out that domestication of animals intensified humans' exploitation of nature far beyond the impact of cooperative labor. The advent of agriculture went still further, making large areas of their habitat unsuitable for many of the plants and animals that had formerly lived in it:

The respect for the habitat of plants and animals that had been necessary for hunter-gatherers was no longer essential in agricultural societies; planting and harvesting disrupted that bond with nature.

This fundamental alteration in humanity's relationship with the habitat of other creatures was accompanied by another equally important change. The eighteenth-century French Enlightenment philosopher Jean-Jacques Rousseau (1712–1778) identified one aspect of it when he wrote in his famous *Discourse on Inequality* in 1754: "*Le premier, qui ayant enclos un terrain s'avisa de dire 'Ceci est à moi' était le vrai fondateur de la société civile.*" ("The first one who enclosed some land and said 'This is mine' was the real founder of civilization.")

Rousseau focused on the claim of private property in land because in his time land was still the main source of wealth. In fact, the development of agriculture—especially the monoculture of the great river valleys of Egypt, Mesopotamia, India, and China—involved an even more fundamental property claim—the ownership of people, and/or of their cooperative labor. To borrow the title of a 1973 collection of poetry by Leonard Cohen, the energy of slaves (or of serfs or indentured peasants) became the most important source of surplus energy. The culture of the slave-owning ruling classes (or of a landowning aristocracy to whom the serfs or peasants were bound) focused on monumental statements of their absolute power over this vital new source of energy, reinforced by religions that communicated the values of the ruling groups. The environment was increasingly seen as the object of widespread cultivation by large numbers of these oppressed agricultural workers—almost always serfs or peasants, sometimes slaves as well.

With regard to sources of energy, here again ancient Greece provides an interesting variant. Greece was a slave-owning society, although less dependent on slaves than on the labor of the *helots*, who are more comparable to serfs. Ancient Greek thinkers extended their concern with proportion in nature and humanity to develop not only the famous *Geometry* of Euclid, but also the theorems of Pythagoras and many other empirical studies of the natural world. They even applied their science and mathematics to practical ends, but because they had a ready supply of energy in the labor of the helots and slaves, there was no incentive to develop new energy technologies (despite the etymology of the word "technology," which comes from the ancient Greek root *techne*). In Roman times, the Greek scientist Hero of Alexandria (10–70 CE) published no fewer than seventy-eight inventions, including plans for a rotary steam engine, but its potential was not grasped as anything more than a child's toy. Thus the availability of a stable source of energy in the form of helot or slave labor made it unnecessary to develop the steam engine any further. Much the same could be said of our dependence on oil today—it is a readily available and secure form of energy, so long as the current geopolitical systems remain in place and the environmental damage can be ignored.

A vital technology for the Greeks was navigation. Travel—classically exemplified in ancient Greek culture by the quest for the Golden Fleece and Homer's *Odyssey*—was essential for trade, for establishing each city-state's initially dependent colonies, and for conquest, throughout the Mediterranean and the Black Sea. The surplus energy required was derived partly from improvements in ship design to take advantage of natural forms of energy like wind and tide—but the Greeks were still reliant on the energy of helots, slaves, or conscripts to row these great boats.

The Romans took over much of Greek culture, systematizing Greek architecture and developing Greek aquatic management techniques into their own sophisticated engineering systems of aqueducts and heated baths. Nevertheless, after establishment of the empire by Augustus (63 BCE–14 CE), their own reliance on the energy of slaves (more so than in ancient Greece) predictably led to a culture preoccupied with impressive monuments and tombs, as well as the lavish physical culture (or lifestyle) of emperors and their appointees, so that their advanced technology remained a secondary source of energy. Traditional Roman religion and some of the new "mystery" religions continued to justify the social-political culture dominated by the emperor's divine right to rule.

The acceptance of Christianity as an official religion in the Roman Empire, especially after the reign of Constantine (272–337 CE), challenged these imperial values. Christian recognition of the worth of each individual accorded with a major change in the western empire's social-political culture that had occurred about a century before Constantine's conversion— the granting of citizenship by Caracalla (188–217 CE), who reigned from 211 to 216, to all freedmen in the empire, including persons of diverse ethnic or colonial backgrounds, especially those who had served in the Roman Army. Many—even some who had started life as slaves—could become Roman citizens. Colonial Roman soldiers of all ethnic backgrounds, even mercenaries from outside the *limes,* became an increasingly important source of surplus energy for the Roman Army in the latter days of the empire; after their useful service many of these veterans were settled on *latifundia,* with substantial landownership for officers and a feudal relationship of fealty to their former commanders for the rank and file, which became the basis for the agricultural economy of medieval Europe. The underlying Roman concept of citizenship as an attribute that is not determined by birthright was revived by the Enlightenment and is vital to the global patterns of immigration that we know today.

The literary aesthetic culture of the latter days of the empire was brilliantly analyzed by the German Jewish philologist Erich Auerbach (1892–1957), who completed his masterful thesis entitled *Mimesis: The Representation of Reality in Western Literature* in Istanbul in 1946, after a decade of exile from Hitler's Germany. Although it ranges from Homer (c. 900 BCE) to Marcel Proust (1871–1922) and Virginia Woolf (1882–1941), *Mimesis* is particularly effective in showing how Latin literary syntax deteriorated in the latter days of the empire. Whereas military dispatches, letters, histories, and senatorial speeches alike during the heyday of the empire had employed the full stock of Latin's subordinate clauses (which Auerbach calls *hypotaxis*) to make sense of events and to put people and things in order of relative importance, in the years of decline they become mere conjunctions of "one thing after another" (*parataxis*—and . . . , and . . . , and . . .). So we witness the declining confidence in the imperial order of things and people, as both writers and readers address each successive phenomenon without structural connectivity to their status or importance. The relative leveling of people and events may be attractive (Ernest Hemingway would have liked it), in contrast to the earlier writings' hierarchies that are characteristic of all ancient empires; this leveling might be related to the introduction of the concept of citizenship that is not dependent on one's place of birth or social status. But it is not hard to see that the empire must soon fall so that new forces of patronage—the church and the former officers who are now lords of the land—could reorder the relative significance of things and people, in both northern and Mediterranean Europe.

In northern climates especially, the warmth of a fire is essential to maintain life through the winter. In northern China, Korea, Japan, and central Asia, in North America, and throughout Europe north of the Mediterranean coast, the source of energy for the hearth was a critical question. This widespread need was met throughout the northern hemisphere by cutting and burning the wood of the temperate zone forests. The power of emperors, kings, and nobles was rooted in their control of the forests—which were being cleared for agriculture while simultaneously being chopped for firewood. Feudal estates maintained large numbers of serfs who were dispersed throughout the land, chopping and delivering the wood to the hearths of castles, cities, and cottages alike and then farming the land after clearing it.

Serfs must feed and reproduce themselves, and the obligation of the ruling classes is to provide a social-political culture within which this is more or less possible. Wood-burning as an energy source made serfdom practical so long as there was an elaborate set of regulations permitting serfs and peasants to collect the discarded bits of wood for firewood in certain areas at certain times to keep themselves warm. Likewise, they were usually allowed to conduct subsistence farming. Wood as a source of energy thus provided a basis for the social-political culture of serfdom, which is a more cost-effective form of labor than slavery.

Perhaps the most moving representations of the meaning of wood energy are the much later paintings by Jean-François Millet (1814–1875) and Vincent van Gogh (1853–1890) of nineteenth-century peasants (not serfs) gathering scraps of wood for firewood. By that date, coal and coke had replaced wood as the primary source of energy, and peasants were being forced off the land into mines and factories by a combination of deforestation and other factors removing them from the land. These heart-breaking paintings and drawings are an example of what Marshall McLuhan (1911–1980) called "the rearview mirror"—one technology has replaced another, putting the old technology in the rearview mirror where it may be seen as the content of works of art by perceptive painters like Millet and Van Gogh.

Jean-François Millet (1814–1875), *Wood Choppers*, c. 1850, black chalk and watercolor on paper, 46.9 x 30.8 cm (18½ x 12⅛ in.), National Galleries of Scotland, purchased 1919. Photo: National Gallery of Scotland.

Wood-burning fire had been an important source of energy for almost all ancient societies. The religion of Zoroastrianism arose in ancient Persia with fire as a symbol of the divine, and the ancient Greek myth of Prometheus as the hero forever tortured on a mountain in the Caucasus because he stole fire from the gods has stayed with us through the millennia. But the absolute dependence on firewood to maintain civilized society through the winter was (and in many places still is) a distinctive characteristic of northern peoples.

The need to burn wood to keep warm, as well as to clear fields for crops, may have been a factor in the mysterious collapse of the Moundbuilder cultures of North America. It appears very likely that these cultures, characterized by ceremonial or serpentine mounds, which ranged from the Great Lakes to the Gulf of Mexico and flourished in various widespread locations from the Archaic period (c. 3400 BCE) through to the fourteenth or fifteenth century CE, were in some way connected to the comparable, but much more fully developed cultures centered in what is now Mexico City. Sensitively worked shell gorgets originating from the Gulf and beautifully crafted sheets of mica are among the evidence for their developed design sense and their far-flung trading connections.

One significant difference between these northern cultures and those far to the south in Mexico was the northern dependence on firewood for fuel. Burning wood for a campfire for a few hundred people within a palisade of saplings around a group of communal longhouses (as was common among the Iroquoian and other agricultural North American cultures) is one thing; but in some places these Moundbuilder cultures grew very large and had to support an urban population. The Mississippian Moundbuilder culture built the city of Cahokia, the largest urban center north of Mexico at the time, with an estimated population of around 10,000 people at its zenith, on the east bank of the Mississippi River opposite what is today St. Louis. The flat-topped pyramidal Monk's Mound at Cahokia is over 30 meters (100 ft) high. It appears to have been the center of a social-political culture that was supported by a monoculture of maize for many miles around the city in southern Illinois. Yet relatively suddenly, over three or four generations in the thirteenth and fourteenth centuries, the city was abandoned and its culture collapsed; one of the reasons may have been that they had cleared so much of the forest to fuel their urban civilization that they became vulnerable to flooding from the Mississippi River and its tributaries and could no longer sustain the ruling groups who are believed to have officiated at ceremonies on the mounds. Cutting and burning wood is

Lloyd K. Townsend, rendering of construction of "Woodhenge," c. 1150 CE, now Cahokia Mounds State Historic Site, Collinsville, Illinois. Photo: Cahokia Mounds State Historic Site.

destructive to the environment and if practiced on a large scale without reforestation can render a society unsustainable.

One link that we maintain with the European cultures associated with burning wood as a source of energy is the Celtic ritual of a communal fire that has come down to us as Hallowe'en. Celtic-speaking people first become evident to archaeologists with a culture based on mining and metallurgy from around the eighth century BCE in what is now southern Germany, Austria, and Switzerland, but over the centuries, until their definitive defeat in France by Julius Caesar, Celts (aka Gauls) also established the dominant cultures of France, northern Italy, England, Wales, Ireland, and parts of Scotland; by intermarriage with the indigenous Iberians throughout what is today Spain (especially Galicia) and Portugal; and into much of central and eastern Europe, even establishing an outpost started by Celtic mercenaries and their families in Turkey (the recipients of St. Paul's *Epistle to the Galatians* in the New Testament). Long after the Roman conquest Celts remained the distinctive people and culture of these countries, known to archaeologists in that period as Gallo-Romans.

Although they did not have their own written culture before contact with Greeks and Romans, Celts did observe an agricultural calendar that began at their New Year's festival of *Samhain* (November 1) and ended the year after harvest, on October 31. As we know, astronomically there are 365 + ¼ days in the year, which we accommodate by accumulating an extra "leap year" day every fourth year; the Celts handled this extra six hours in their annual calendar by declaring the last six hours of October 31 to be a separate time period outside the calendar, during which all spirits were loose and when ribald, licentious, or otherwise antisocial behavior would therefore be tolerated. To maintain social unity during this potentially dangerous period, some Celtic groups practiced a ritual of lighting a communal bonfire, to which each household brought a pot, gourd, or other container in order to return home with a few embers to light their own hearths, once again bonding their family with the larger group for another year.

As the Celts were Christianized, their priests could not forbid this popular custom, so they transformed this somewhat threatening "all spirits' evening" into All Hallows' Eve (meaning the evening before All Saints' Day), when all the hallowed saints would be about, instead of heathen spirits. Mischief was to be limited to the children on what we now know as Hallowe'en. We may no longer know either the spirits or the saints, but the ritual of lighting a few embers of the communal fire in a gourd has been maintained in our time in the form of a jack o'lantern, a leering face carved into a pumpkin with a candle inside, a sign that the house in front of which it gleams is participating once again in the annual communal ritual of Hallowe'en. Celtic languages are still spoken in parts of Brittany, Wales, Scotland, and Ireland, but Ireland is where Celtic culture has been best preserved; flying into Dublin on October 31 some years ago, Barry looked down from the plane to see communal bonfires burning in each village across the landscape. The values of burning wood as a source of surplus energy are still with us.

Fairy tales of many societies about woodcutters and children in the forest are among other cultural records of the dependence on burning wood as the source of energy for warmth in the northern winter. Still more are to be seen in the depictions of woodcutters, peasants, and other forest people in paintings, such as the devotional *Books of Hours* of the Middle Ages or the landscapes glimpsed through the windows of Flemish paintings of the fifteenth and sixteenth centuries. In some of these pictures we can also notice the technological developments of medieval Europe—the horse's bit, the stirrup, and developments of the plow and plowshare—that made the peasants' work on the cleared fields more productive and further intensified the exploitation of the environment. Windmills and watermills also provided other energy sources, used for milling the grain from the harvest by means of millstones. But the overriding need of the feudal nobles was to preserve their rights to cut down trees and to replace forests with fields as they pleased on their inherited lands. In England in 1215 these landowning lords forced King John (1167–1216) to sign a charter guaranteeing their rights over their *demesnes*—which was the original intent of the *Magna Charta*, now seen by many as the first document of human rights and parliamentary democracy in Great Britain. At the medieval castle in the English city of Lincoln, Barry consulted with its keepers on planning the display of one of the few extant copies of this document, which has also been the subject of international blockbuster traveling exhibitions in America. This record of social-political culture has had a far-reaching effect on all other types of culture, including the aesthetic.

Belgian historian Henri Pirenne (1862–1935) dated the significant growth of European cities from around 1250, although he and the great French historian Fernand Braudel (1902–1985) documented extensive trade as the source of urban development much earlier in medieval Europe. Over the following centuries, the pace and volume of mercantile exchange and urbanization substantially increased, with concomitant demands for an energy source to heat the homes of the merchants and other city dwellers who had no land of their own. By the seventeenth century, global trading cities like Amsterdam made still greater demands, and by the eighteenth century, Paris, London, and other urban centers required still larger supplies of wood for heating and other energy needs.

Yet as the people of the Durance River valley knew, the merchant and military navies of the emerging nation-states demanded even more from Europe's forests. The ships of the great age of sail depended on wind power for energy, but they were built of cut wood. While the *radeliers* at Embrun supplied the French Navy, the British built their still larger fleet with timber first from Norway, then from Russia, and—after Napoleon's invasion endangered that source—from the forests of New Brunswick. That colony's capital, Saint John, became the world's shipyard, as British vessels from around the globe anchored in its harbor at the mouth of the Saint John River to repair or replace broken masts or spars with new wood from the still productive forests of northern New Brunswick in what is now Canada. The collection of the New

Unknown Easter Island artist, bifacial head, prior to 1843 (the year before it was donated to the Mechanic's Institute in exchange for free admission by the crew of the ship *Margaret Rait,* who had recently been to Easter Island and whose ship was in dock for repairs in Saint John harbor), painted *tapa* (reeds, barkcloth, and wood), 20.3 x 19.7 x 19.7 cm (8 x 7¾ x 7¾ in.), New Brunswick Museum, Saint John (1979.126.2). Photo: New Brunswick Museum.

Brunswick Museum includes artifacts from as far away as Easter Island, which are particularly valuable to researchers because they are dated to the day when sailors brought them to the museum to get free admission for a visit, while waiting for their vessels to be repaired.

In China there was originally a parallel development to European navigation as the great Admiral Zheng He (c. 1371–1435) set sail for the Indies in 1405 with no fewer than 317 vessels. Sources claim that three hundred acres of forest were felled for each of his large "treasure ships" alone—although this may be an exaggeration, it is still obvious that there must have been extensive clear-cutting for such an immense fleet of masted vessels. Zheng He went on to make seven epochal voyages until 1433, each with a large fleet, sailing through the islands of southeast Asia to reach as far as what is today Sri Lanka, both east and west coasts of India, and the shores of East Africa. In the main Chinese shipyard city of Nanjing—then the world's largest shipbuilding center—the construction or refit of 1,681 vessels is recorded in the three years 1406–1408 alone. But just as the Greeks could not see the potential of a steam engine due to the ready availability of slave labor, so the Chinese emperors of both the Ming and subsequent Qing dynasties decided that Zheng He's journeys were too expensive and too destructive of their forests. They welcomed the exotic specimens such as giraffes that he brought back for the emperor's private zoo, but they had no interest in the potential of trade with the rest of Asia and Africa, because they were reliant on the feudal energy of their indentured peasants, who produced the agricultural wealth of the empire, as administered by their famed civil servants. By the late 1430s—just as the Portuguese were extending their history-making probes along the coast of Africa—the emperor ordered an end to such voyages, and by the 1500s a series of decrees made it illegal for anyone to build or sail a seaworthy ocean-going vessel with multiple masts. The Qing emperors went further, forcibly removing the population from a seven-hundred-mile strip of China's southern coast, so that the "Middle Kingdom" became entirely reliant on its internal resources.

In Europe, by contrast, the great age of wooden ships for trade and for the navies to defend the far-flung trade routes demanded the harvest of more and more forests, throughout the continent and then worldwide. Together with the demand for firewood and the continuing need to clear fields for planting, the depredation of the forests effectively denuded Europe of its forest cover. A case can be made that by the end of the eighteenth century, or certainly by the first quarter of the nineteenth, Western Europe had cut down so much of its forests that it simply had to go below ground to find the energy it needed. In other words, viewed from the standpoint of energy sources, the Industrial Revolution may not have been so much a triumphant accomplishment of manufacturing capital, as it was a desperate necessity.

Whether by choice or due to necessity, by the mid-nineteenth century a new source of energy—digging and burning coal—had come to dominate most of European and North American society, and to affect much of the rest of the world as well. This time the invention of the steam engine (by James Watt[1] in eighteenth-century England) was recognized for its transformative potential, and the development of the steam locomotive, the steamboat, and steam-powered manufacturing mills of all kinds realized many of the possible applications of coal as an energy source. The effects on the environment, and on social organization, required to mine the coal, burn it, and use its energy in the factories of the nineteenth century, were devastating.

Capitalists and the first communists alike could see that this powerful, transforming source of energy depended on the concentration and organization of large numbers of workers—originally including women and children, but later limited to men—to go down into dark, often dangerous mines to bring up the coal that was the source of all other wealth in the new manufacturing economy. This kind of labor was very different from that of dispersed woodcutters in the forests or serfs working the fields of feudal nobles: in order to maximize the profit to be drawn from the mines, these workers had to be tightly controlled, very often on rotating shifts day and night. As so often, religion reinforced the values needed for social control: as the British economic historian R. H. Tawney (1880–1962) pointed out in his 1926 book *Religion and the Rise of Capitalism*, Protestant (especially Calvinist) religious teachings reinforced the idea that value derives from hard work—an underlying assumption shared by mine or factory owners and union organizers in all mining and manufacturing areas, whatever the religion of the miners or factory workers.

Social-political culture responded from the early 1800s forward, first with the "utopian" socialist philosophies of thinkers like Joseph Fourier (1768–1830), le Comte de Saint-Simon (1760–1825), and Pierre-Joseph Proudhon (1809–1865) in France and Robert Owen (1771–1858) in Scotland, then with the more "scientific" socialism and the *Communist Manifesto* of 1848 by Karl Marx (1818–1883) and Friedrich Engels (1820–1895). Aesthetic culture reflected the change most directly in the most popular art form of the nineteenth century—the novel—especially in England, the heartland of the Industrial Revolution, with such works as Charles Dickens's *Hard Times*, Elizabeth Gaskell's *Mary Barton*, and Benjamin Disraeli's *Sybil, or the Two Nations*.[2] In France, Emile Zola (1840–1902) went much further with his twenty-volume series published from 1871 to 1893 chronicling the fortunes of the Rougon-Macquart family, especially in *Germinal* (1885), set in the mining country of northern France.

Besides the subject matter of novels, there were more subtle responses to the new valuation of work as the source of value. Russian author Anton

Chekhov's five great plays produced by Konstantin Stanislavsky (1863–1938) around the turn of the twentieth century all feature characters who invoke the virtues of work. Sonya in *Uncle Vanya*, for instance, forced to recognize that her love for the Doctor is unrequited and condemned therefore to live out her life beside her uncle managing a barely sustainable estate, ends the play (first produced in 1899) with a prayer and the mantra, "We must work, we must work." Although these vague appeals to work are often ironic—as they were to Chekhov (1860–1904) when he heard them—they express the emerging conviction, soon shared by capitalist and communist alike, that organized work is the source of all value, as it had become the primary source of energy for all. This idea was put into practice on Henry Ford's automobile production lines in Detroit in the early twentieth century, and after 1917 it became the ethos of a major change in the social-political culture of Russia.

The new material culture of industrial manufacturing of course had the capacity to produce far larger numbers of products of all kinds, and to ship and sell them around the globe. Britain was called the world's workshop (as China is today). The manufacturing capitalists' patronage initially produced large numbers of objects designed to follow decorative patterns unrelated to the new methods of production or to the new needs of the working population. Industrial designers responded in two ways:

- The great British designer William Morris (1834–1896) led the way initially back to medieval values of handmade objects, the opposite of what was now possible with factory production. Later, Morris established a company to fabricate products such as his famous wallpapers in sufficient quantity to appeal to patrons with the discrimination to favor his more sensitively designed commodities. The Arts and Crafts Movement, which favored such preindustrial values, affected a large number of architects, ceramists, and cabinetmakers in England and America, reacting against the manufacturing ethos even when their designs were mass-produced. Around the turn of the twentieth century, art nouveau buildings, furniture, and textiles reacted against mechanization with sinuous organic designs rooted in nature.
- A contrasting movement, beginning in England with Christopher Dresser (1834–1904), began to design directly for mass production with an eye to the *function* of the objects. On the European continent, the Wiener Werkstatte in Vienna, Jugendstil in Germany and the Netherlands, and other movements took this direction of industrial design forward until it culminated in Germany between the two world

Aiming to retain traditional qualities of the artisan during the Industrial Revolution: William Morris (1834–1896), "Rossetti" arm-chair, designed for Pre-Raphaelite artist Dante Gabriel Rossetti (1828–1882), manufactured 1870–1890, painted ebonized beech with rush seat, 88.8 x 49.5 x 53 cm (35 x 19½ x 21 in.), Victoria and Albert Museum, London. Photo: V&A Images/Art Resource, NY.

Designing to use industrial manufacturing processes to meet functional requirements: Ludwig Mies van der Rohe (1886–1969), prototype of Barcelona-Sessel chair, 1929, chrome-plated steel and leather, 78 x 66.2 x 83.3 cm (30¾ x 26 x 32¾ in.), Design Collection Torsten Bröhan, Berlin. Photo: Torsten Bröhan.

wars at the Bauhaus, the distinctive design school of the twentieth century. When the Nazis ended the patronage of that school in 1933, they forced the emigration of the world's leading architects, designers, and design instructors throughout the world, especially to America, where they found responsive patrons who helped them to create the world of modern architecture and design that we are all living in today.

Meanwhile, Charlie Chaplin (1889–1977) had forever epitomized the industrial worker comedically in his 1936 film *Modern Times*. The Soviet

Union had turned from the constructivism of its revolutionary period to socialist realism in the visual arts and literature, focused on the "pathetic grandeur" of the worker. As Russians read the novels of Maxim Gorky (1868–1936) and watched the films of Sergei Eisenstein (1898–1948) and Vsevolod Pudovkin (1893–1953) in the first two decades of their revolution, so after 1949 the Chinese revolutionary government patronized the populist stories of Lu Hsun (1881–1936) and works of art like the powerfully evocative sculptural environment entitled *The Rent Collection Courtyard*, focused on the preindustrial labor of the peasants. All of this aesthetic culture was rooted in the conviction that value and meaning spring from labor.

Yet it was gradually becoming evident on both sides of what Winston Churchill in 1947 called the "Iron Curtain," that this socioeconomic culture based on coal as the prime source of energy for manufacturing was deleterious to the environment. As early as 1845, Friedrich Engels's indictment, *The Condition of the Working Class in England*, depicted the horrendous effects of Manchester's textile mills on England's polluted rivers and canals, as well as on the lives of the men and women drawn into the world's first great industrial city to work in them. At the opposite end of the ideological spectrum, Thomas Carlyle's book *Past and Present* contrasted what life and the landscape of England had been like before the Industrial Revolution with what it was already becoming by the mid-nineteenth century. As the rest of the world industrialized in turn, these terrible conditions and the misery associated with them were perpetuated worldwide. The manufacturing bourgeoisie had little concern for the environmental effects, as well as the devastating social impact, of the source of the surplus energy that generated their profits.

In the early twentieth century, the discovery and development of ways to transform waterpower into electricity initially appeared to offer a cleaner, less damaging alternative energy source. Despite the awesome power of the turbines at sites like Niagara Falls, however, the most widely used source of electrical energy has become once again the burning of coal. As journalist Fareed Zakaria points out in his 2008 book *The Post-American World* (published by W. W. Norton & Co.), "between 2006 and 2012, China and India will build eight hundred new coal-fired (electrical) power plants—with combined CO_2 emissions five times the total savings of the Kyoto accords." Statistically—and more important, environmentally—burning coal remains the world's largest source of energy at the outset of the twenty-first century.

Despite this fact, the development of another new energy source has been decisive in affecting our values—the discovery of effective ways to use oil and natural gas for surplus energy. Having established Canada's first Natural History Museum—now part of the New Brunswick Museum—in the wooden ship repair center of Saint John in 1842, geologist and chemist Abraham Gesner (1797–1864) moved back to his native Nova Scotia, where he developed a practical means of making kerosene, a usable source of light and energy, from oil. By the mid-nineteenth century, "jerker rods" were pumping oil from fields in Ontario and Pennsylvania, and in 1901 the first oil strike was made at a salt dome called Spindletop in Texas. Over the next half-century, burning oil and natural gas was to replace coal as the source of surplus energy that mattered most. By 1940, a century after Gesner, the struggle to control sources of oil had become a major motivation for conquest in World War II—for Nazi Germany to invade the Soviet Union to reach the oil fields around Baku and for the Japanese to gain control of the offshore oil of Indonesia, especially after the United States had imposed an embargo on oil exports to the island nation, which had no oil of its own. Oil remains a significant factor in most of the major conflicts of our own time.

The effects on our values have been far-reaching, although seldom understood until now. The *zeitgeist* of the age of oil and gas differs radically from that of the age of coal:

- Most significantly, it is no longer obvious that value derives from work. Neither the discovery nor the exploitation of oil or natural gas requires such great concentrations of organized labor. Finding, drilling, and transporting the energy source are in themselves relatively clean activities, and in comparison with coal mining they can be accomplished with far fewer workers to produce a far greater amount of energy. Value no longer appears so obviously to arise from the concentration of large numbers of organized workers. This is not a difference in material reality, but a vast shift in the *perception* of where value comes from.
- Instead, the nexus of value appears to rest much more on the *markets* for oil and gas. Whereas the concerns of the owners of coal mines in the nineteenth and early twentieth centuries very often had to be focused on the stubborn struggles of the miners to improve their working conditions, those who control the oil and gas sector are far less likely to be concerned with their workforce, but do need to monitor the markets for their products, and the prices they are able to obtain—as the minutes of OPEC meetings attest. The focus of perceived value shifts to the opposite end of the spectrum—the consumption of energy by their customers, the security of transporting the energy via pipelines and tankers,

and the sophisticated technologies and logistics required to ensure cost effective extraction and delivery of this resource. The oil and gas workforce is more knowledge-based than labor-based.

Once again, we must remember that the changes in values associated with new sources of energy are additive. Statistically, coal remains an important energy source, and the values of work associated with it are still very much with us. Nevertheless, the cultural change that results from the reorientation associated with oil is so far-reaching and so familiar to us that it is hard to articulate, but may be sensed to some extent by the ways in which the culture of Texas differs from that of the rest of the United States, or the culture of Alberta differs from the rest of Canada. Some would say that those who control the wells in these oil-producing areas are more "materialistic," whereas the difference really consists in their perception that value derives from the delivery and purchase of their products, not primarily from the actual production process. *Marketing* and *logistics* have become an important component of the social-political and aesthetic cultures of the oil and gas era.

The nature of this cultural change may be grasped much more fully in the heartlands of the oil- and gas-producing countries, such as Saudi Arabia or the small but dynamic countries of the Arabian (formerly Persian) Gulf. Oil was discovered here starting in the 1930s in Bahrain. At first this energy resource was controlled by the north Atlantic powers—U.S., Dutch, and British petroleum companies. During the great era of decolonization in the 1960s and 1970s, the Arabian Gulf countries themselves and their ruling monarchies wrested control of their energy industry through negotiation and in some cases through nationalization. The result is that each of these countries has a highly sophisticated market-, logistics-, and technology-oriented national energy company as its economic base.

Saudi Arabia, which has the largest proven reserves, also has the largest population among these countries, consisting mainly of young people. However, its cultural activities are highly controlled by its ultra-conservative religious leaders, who insist on religious content dominating all public schools and forbid cinema and theater, censor books, and retain control over public education such that Saudi Arabian education ranks 93rd of 129, behind Albania, the Philippines, Peru, and Tajikistan, in the 2008 UNESCO global index assessing quality of education.[3] This poor performance is astonishing considering the country's wealth and dangerous considering the pressure from the large population of young men seeking to enter a job market for which they are not likely to be qualified. Nonetheless, cautious efforts are being made by the oil company Saudi Aramco and King Abdullah to bring the country into the knowledge age. In 2009, the country launched King Abdullah University of Science and Technology (KAUST), its first coeducational high-tech university, which has attracted scientists from around the world.

At this writing, Gail is leading a multidisciplinary team of Lord Cultural Resources consultants in assisting Aramco to create the King Abdul Aziz Center for Knowledge and Culture, called iTHRA in Arabic, at Dhahran in the Eastern Province of Saudi Arabia. The intent of this future-oriented project—designed by the Norwegian architectural firm, Snohetta—is to establish a global monument to learning and cultural exchange inspiring civic society, creativity, and bridging to the knowledge economy. This cultural project is unique in the Gulf not only for its courage in the face of religious conservatism, but because the leadership will be Saudis themselves—talented men and women who have been educated through the Aramco schools and foreign universities and who have a sophisticated understanding of the marketing, communications, engineering, logistics, and technology of the oil industry. Our task is to impart our knowledge of planning and managing cultural institutions to this group and to collaborate with them to build a twenty-first-century cultural center that includes theater, cinemas, museums, galleries, and a children's discovery zone. During planning sessions in Oslo, Toronto, and Dhahran, Gail has often thought about the intersection of the three oil cultures: her country, Canada (which is the number two oil producer in the world after Saudi Arabia); Norway (number eight and a relative newcomer to this energy source), where the architects are based; and Saudi Arabia, which is the site of the project and is number one.

Other Gulf states on the Arabian peninsula have huge oil or natural gas wealth but tiny populations, so the per capita wealth created by the energy source far exceeds that of Canada, Norway, and Saudi Arabia together. Several of these—especially Qatar and the United Arab Emirates—have decided to use this wealth to enter the knowledge economy—leading with culture, shopping, and higher education. All these countries are investing in the social-political culture related to present and future energy sources, particularly in engineering and earth sciences—because they are intensely aware that oil and natural gas are finite resources, and they are actively engaged not only with the discovery process of new finds worldwide, but also investing in alternative energy sources.

Because individual wealth in these countries is very great and most of the labor is imported by immigrants who will not be given an opportunity to become citizens, these are oil and gas cultures that find value much more in consumption than in production and have a keen interest in marketing and successful commercial *brands*. Like all good customers, they like acquiring branded products and enjoy their acquisitions. As the Emirates have begun to develop a museum culture, they are doing so by leasing brands like the Louvre or the Guggenheim, while wisely deploying their wealth to acquire outstanding works of art. As the great museums of western Europe and America were enriched by the profits of the coal mining and manufacturing age, so the new museums of the Arabian Gulf are being stocked by works borrowed or purchased with the wealth derived from oil and natural gas; but the contrasting values of the coal and oil age can also be discerned in the different ways in which these museum systems have been built. Whereas the robber barons of the coal era plundered the globe by imperial conquest to bring back great works of art and artifacts from colonized civilizations, the sheikhs and emirs of the age of oil and gas are purchasing their collections at auction or through dealers on the open market.

In this process, there is great significance for all humanity. Just two generations ago, these societies were mainly nomadic, centered in fishing villages and trading in commodities like pearls. In two generations, the people of the Gulf have traversed 5,000 to 10,000 years of development. Just a decade ago, very little of the region's Islamic heritage actually existed in the region. It was almost entirely in the great private and public collections of the north Atlantic countries. Led by the Kuwaiti and Qatari royal families, some of the great works from many Islamic countries have recently been purchased and returned to their regional context. Now and in the future, scholars, connoisseurs, and most importantly local people will be able to view the arts of Islam and the Arabic world in this region, most notably in the magnificent Qatar Museum of Islamic Art designed by the Chinese-American architect I. M. Pei, with the galleries and their furnishings by the French exhibition designer, Jean-Michel Wilmotte.

An aesthetic culture of the oil and gas era that recognizes value in marketing is all around us. Many observers, still steeped in the work-centered values of the age of coal, have deplored the extent to which marketing now affects all aspects of our aesthetic culture, not only in fashion, design, pop music, movies, TV, or video games, but also extends increasingly to the "fine art" cultures of classical music, theater, opera, architecture, and museums. *Because awareness of their markets is critical to the leading sources of patronage at a time when oil and gas are the key sources of surplus energy, our aesthetic culture today at all levels prizes market values and often presents all aspects of contemporary culture as the "brands" of particular artists or cultural institutions.*

I. M. Pei, architect, bridge to the main entrance of the Qatar Museum of Islamic Art, Doha, 2008. Photo: Christian Waltl.

Hence the architectural style of new cultural buildings is seen as a marketing opportunity—a way to establish a new "brand" for the cultural institution, a city, or a region. *Museo Guggenheim Bilbao* is the best-known example, but there are many more, and a whole generation of architects has responded with imaginative structures that go far beyond their basic functional program to establish the newly conceived *content* of the museum, concert hall, or theater. Even renovations of historic structures are aimed at revitalizing the content of the cultural institution. An emphasis on the style of visual artists and the "star system" for performing artists are equally consequences of the preoccupation with marketing and brands that comes with the age of oil and gas.

Another important cultural effect of the oil and gas era is the transfer of value from labor to *credit*. When our grandparents wanted a washing machine or a refrigerator, they worked and saved until they could afford to buy one; even if they bought a product on a "lay away" basis, they didn't acquire or enjoy their purchase until it was fully paid for. Trade has always involved some extension of credit, but the ubiquity of credit for all consumers is the cultural change that has made it possible for almost all of us to participate much more quickly in the acquisition and consumption of material goods—the focus of value in the age of oil and gas. Famously, credit for all was spurred on by the automobile industry—directly dependent on oil as its source of energy—as Henry Ford and others began to sell cars in the first quarter of the twentieth century with payments "on time."

Although the Great Depression slowed this development, after World War II buying on time but getting the product right away became the norm in Western industrial countries. Oil companies issued the first credit cards for service at their gasoline (petrol) stations. Today we pay for almost everything with credit cards made of plastic—another oil product. Companies pay their employees' wages with a "line of credit" held against the firms' future revenues. The stability of the U.S. economy is increasingly dependent on the sale of Treasury Bonds—a form of credit—to other countries, especially China and Japan, while the U.S. dollar is sustained by its status as the world's "petrodollar," the currency of oil. Bankers seek customers to extend credit to them even if their means are very modest, and financial "assets" are created out of debts—sometimes to a fault, as the financial crisis of 2008–2009 revealed, when the greed of some banks and investment brokers for ever greater profits extended credit to too many who could not pay. Thus:

> *The age of oil and gas as the crucial source of surplus energy requires widespread social acceptance and understanding of the value of marketing, branding, and credit. What these relatively abstract concepts have in common is that they are all future-oriented.*

Markets and the relative appeal of brands are always changing—think of Coca Cola, "Classic Coke," and now "Zero Coke"—and the goal of marketing campaigns is always to affect those changes in ways that will be positive for the patrons of the campaigns. "The next big thing" is what marketing and branding is about, and credit offers the only way in which most of us will be able to pay for it.

> *Paradoxically, it is this very awareness of the need to find value in perceived future possibilities, with a view to their marketability and their potential to sustain the debt that their development will incur, that has led to our environmental consciousness today.*

In the age of coal the horrendous depredation of the environment was obvious to everyone, but the mine-owners and manufacturers didn't care as long as they made their profits, and few of the rest of us cared because we believed that all value derived from work, so the results of that work justified whatever effects it might have on the environment. In the age of oil and gas, with its focus on the value of marketing and the credit necessary to be able to acquire the products that this surplus energy makes possible, we are deeply concerned with what the future may hold—what effects it will have on future markets and on the debt that will be needed to sustain not only the development under consideration, but also the national, corporate, or individual customers whose purchases will eventually enable the indebted developers to pay back the loans without which the development cannot take place. This was again made clear during the credit crisis of 2008–2009, when developers—including developers of cultural projects—could not obtain the credit they needed to continue their projects, even in Dubai.

So the age of oil and gas has made us conscious of the effects of everything we do on the future, specifically on the future of the environment, because the value nexus of the culture of this era is focused on perceived future possibilities and limitations, not on exploitative mining. Thus the Alberta Tar Sands development may serve our oil or gas needs today, but will its effects on the environment be so dysfunctional that it will impact the ability of companies and consumers to pay back the credit that is necessary for its present development?

Having oil and gas as a primary source of surplus energy has forced us to become environmentally conscious because of the future-oriented sense of values that comes with this energy source.

The awesome images that Canadian photographer Edward Burtynsky takes of our "manufactured landscapes" (also the title of a documentary film about his work) evoke precisely this paradox. Especially the large-scale color photographs in his 2009 exhibition entitled simply *Oil* at the Corcoran Gallery of Art in Washington, DC, at once reveal the devastation caused by oil and gas around the world, find a terrible beauty in it, and simultaneously force us to recognize that this destruction of our planet and its resources must stop if we are to have a future. Providing an outstanding example of how a creative artist initiates the awareness of new content, thereby attracting a new level of patronage, Burtynsky himself describes his discovery of the power of these stupendous and horrifying images in the preface to the book (also entitled *Oil*, published by Steidl in Göttingen, Germany) that accompanied his Corcoran exhibition:

> I began to think about oil itself: as both the source of energy that makes everything possible, and as a source of dread, for its ongoing endangerment of our habitat.
>
> In 1997 I had what I refer to as my oil epiphany. It occurred to me that all the vast man-altered landscapes I had pursued for over 20 years had been made possible by the discovery of oil and the progress occasioned by the internal combustion engine. Over the next 12 years I researched and photographed the largest oil fields I could find. I went on to make images of refineries, freeway interchanges, automobile plants and the scrap industry resulting from the recycling of cars. I began to look at motor culture, where vast tribes come together with vehicles as the main attraction.
>
> In no way can one encompass the influence and extended landscape of this thing we call oil. These images can be seen as notations by one artist—contemplating the world made possible through this massive energy force, and the cumulative effects of the industrial evolution.

Burtynsky's photographs are examples of what the eighteenth century called "the sublime," defined by German philosopher Immanuel Kant (1724–1804) as "an outrage on the imagination." In the nineteenth century the paintings and photographs of nature that were called sublime were romantic evocations of the power of Niagara Falls, the overwhelming magnitude of mountains, or the impassive expanse of the sea. Pioneer French photographer Gustave Le Grey (1820–1882), for example, exhibited powerful but radically simple seascapes in Paris in 1857 that Martin Barnes, a curator at the Victoria & Albert Museum in London, for a show at the V&A over 150 years later could still describe as "breathtaking in their subtlety and symphonic grandeur." But in the age of acute awareness of environmental degradation, a photographer who evokes the beauty and power of nature in that way would appear to be evading or denying what former U.S. vice president Al Gore calls "an uncomfortable truth." Burtynsky confronts that terrible truth, and achieves a new kind of "man-made sublime"—one that simultaneously attracts, repels, and overwhelms us.[4]

The environmental consciousness that Burtynsky's images communicate so powerfully has been further enhanced by our ability to visualize the earth as it exists in space. It is instructive to recall that another pioneer French pho-

Shock and awe at the landscape of oil: Edward Burtynsky, *SOCAR Oil Fields #3, Baku, Azerbaijan*, 2006, color photograph, Nicholas Metivier Gallery, Toronto. Photo: Edward Burtynsky, courtesy of Hasted Hunt Kraeutler Gallery, New York/Nicholas Metivier Gallery, Toronto.

tographer, Felix Nadar (1820–1910), took the first aerial photograph from a balloon in 1858, little more than a century before the first view of the earth from space satellites. In 1999 contemporary French aerial photographer Yann Arthus-Bertrand published the first edition (with Harry N. Abrams, Inc.) of his awesome photographs entitled *Earth from Above*, magnificent images from around the globe that have also been shown worldwide as a touring panel exhibition. Today Google Earth 3.0 allows everyone not only to see but to play with the image of earth in space, to zoom in and out all around the planet. Visual artists are currently responding to this new reality, as scientists try to impress on us all the urgency of the impact of climate change and the need for controls on the kind of exploitation that Burtynsky depicts.

Like aerial photography, environmental art is another of the new directions resulting from the consciousness of meanings arising from our sources of energy today. Because the values associated with diverse energy sources are additive, and since all the energy sources are still with us, it is possible to see evidence of all of them in our world today:

- Cooperative labor remains the defining characteristic of human nature—as finding the best way to maintain it remains our greatest challenge. In aesthetic culture, the need to express the *identity* of the cooperating group remains paramount, and is a central theme of much of the art, music, drama, and literature produced by artists around the world today.
- Slavery or something close to it—near-absolute control over the lives and labor of others assumed by political or religious leaders—unfortunately remains with us in some parts of the world. But it is seldom on a big enough scale to support the monumental sculpture or architecture that usually characterizes the aesthetic culture of such domination.
- We still chop down trees and burn wood in fireplaces. But because this is no longer an essential source of energy in most of the world, the aesthetic culture associated with it has become romantic—or persists in the form of fairy tales for the nursery. Meanwhile we continue to live with the effects of the removal of the forest cover from large parts of the world.
- Windmills and watermills are also now seen as romantic, and are very often restored as heritage centers, which not only evoke their historical function of grinding grain, but in some cases also serve as incubators for new ideas about applying wind and water power to our energy problems today.
- As we noted, burning coal remains statistically the most important source of energy today, due to its use for conversion to electrical power. Social-political and aesthetic cultures based on the value of work are still very much with us. Unfortunately so is the carbon footprint that results from our reliance on coal.
- Despite the persistence of coal-fired electrical power stations, during the past century oil and gas became the crucial new source of surplus energy, and remain so today. The concomitant shift in our sense of the *locus* of values from production to consumption continues to affect us mightily, as we live in a "material world" preoccupied with marketing, brands, and the access to credit that makes it possible for us to acquire its products. Our cultural institutions and many of our artists are deeply affected by and engaged in this value system, and we increasingly per-

ceive an artist's style as his or her personal "brand." At the same time, the preoccupation with the future that is essential to both marketing and debt-management strategies has resulted in a heightened awareness of the effects of our energy choices on the environment—stimulating the environmental consciousness that characterizes so many aspects of our culture today.

Nuclear energy is currently on the agenda. The effect of heightened reliance on nuclear energy as an alternative to exclusive dependence on oil and gas or on coal-fired electricity may be seen first in France, where nuclear energy has been enthusiastically adopted as the solution to long-range energy needs. Although it is too early to draw any conclusions, we may discern several tendencies:

- Certainly nuclear energy requires knowledge workers even more than the oil industry. Not only is French education focused on developing knowledge workers, but also French republican secularism is theoretically aimed at creating a society characterized by "technology, talent, and tolerance," the three Ts that American economist Richard Florida (in such books as *The Rise of the Creative Class*) has suggested are imperative to sustain a knowledge society of creative workers.
- Contemporary French civilization is also strongly reliant on brands, a concern that is evident not only in the fashion industry and in the luxury brand shops, but also in the struggle to protect the "*marques déposées*" of products from cheese to cognac, champagne, and wines. It is worth noting that the process of classifying the types and qualities of French products arose in the scientific age of the *encyclopédistes* of the Enlightenment; it has reached an apogee in the luxury-brand-frenzy world of oil—to such a degree that some of the greatest wealth in France is generated by luxury brands. France itself has become a luxury brand, as it is the number one tourist destination in the world and has retained that position for years. While French artists may be less obviously branded than Americans like Jeff Koons, the Japanese artist Takashi Murakami, the "YBAs" (Young British Artists), or the many highly branded Chinese contemporary artists, some of the leading French patrons—the owners of the great luxury brand houses—are deeply involved in establishing their brands in international contemporary art. In June 2009, while the Louis Vuitton collection of contemporary art was showing at the Hong Kong Art Museum, François Pinault, owner

of Gucci, Yves St. Laurent, Chateau Latour, Balenciaga, and Christie's Auction House (among other brands), opened his new museum at the historic Punta della Dogana, renovated for the purpose by the outstanding Japanese architect Tadao Ando, in Venice. Our French company, Lordculture, which had a minor role in that project, was meanwhile planning museum-quality space to store the collection formed by the myriad of products over the years of the French luxury brand house Hermès.

It would appear that educating knowledge workers; aspiring to a secular, tolerant society; a continued preoccupation with branding; and quite likely the auction houses will all have an important role to play in the patronage of the future, whatever other value shifts nuclear energy may entail.

It is tempting but difficult to go still further to speculate on what effect the widespread adoption of solar or wind power might have on our value system. Barry recently visited the construction site of a new cultural center being built in Aviles in Spain, beside a production center for the big wind-power towers. It is important to remember that any such effects will be additive—the values of the preceding energy sources will stay with us, even as the emerging new values are intuited by the most advanced artists and their patrons.

What this chapter has shown is that our awareness of the changing source of surplus energy has a direct effect on each historical period, including our own, as it results in the acceptance and awareness of values first by the social group that controls access to these sources of energy, but then, in accordance with the principles of cultural change, taken up by the population at large, after these values have been sensed and expressed in their work by the leading artists of the day. This is especially true in the globalized age in which we now live. Our next and final chapter looks at cultural change today.

NOTES

1. Scottish inventor James Watt (1736–1819).

2. Dickens initially published *Hard Times* in serial form in 1854 in his journal, *Household Words*. Here he also published articles by his friend Elizabeth Gaskell (1810–1865). The novel *Mary Barton* was published anonymously in 1848. Benjamin Disraeli (1804–1881) published *Sybil, or the Two Nations* in 1845.

3. Ulf Laessing, "Saudi Education Lags Behind New High-Tech University," Reuters, 15 September 2009.

4. The Burtynsky photograph that we reproduce here was taken in the Baku oil fields, the prize that motivated Adolf Hitler to invade the Soviet Union in 1941.

CHAPTER 9

Contemporary Cultural Change

TEACHING art history is teaching cultural change. In his teaching Barry has found that one way to communicate the pace and sweep of cultural change to students is to ask each one in a class to represent a generation, and to do research to speak for the culture and events of that time period. Assuming an average of twenty-five years per generation, a student down front in the first row would be designated to represent, research, and report on 2010, the student beside her 1985, the third 1960, and so on. It's a valuable didactic exercise for two reasons: on the one hand, the exercise teaches the rapidity and extent of cultural change, especially if the students are asked to report on different issues or in greater depth throughout the course; at the same time the participants discover how few individuals—parents, grandparents, great grandparents, and so on—stand between them and the historic events and shifts in cultural values that they are studying. With a person standing for each generation, only five individuals separate us from the Edwardian days prior to World War I; nine take us back to the heyday of Napoleon, Goya, David, and Beethoven.

Consider just the past two generations alone:

- In 1985, one generation ago, the Internet, which had been invented in 1969, was just getting started as a widespread means of personal and business communication. The fall of the Berlin wall and the dissolution of the Soviet Union were four years away, in 1989. In that year, we worked with a Scottish team that planned to use a computer program called Hypertext to provide public interpretation for *Glasgow's Glasgow*, the centerpiece show for Glasgow's year as European Capital of Culture in 1990; the result was highly controversial, being only the second time that computers had appeared in British museum exhibitions to that date.

- In 1960, two generations ago, only three years had passed since Soviet scientists had sent Sputnik, the first satellite, into space in 1957. A year ago, in 1959, Fidel Castro and his comrades had liberated Cuba from the rule of the dictator Fulgencio Batista (1901–1973). Pop artists were enjoying the response of a few prescient collectors to their first group exhibitions. Secretaries typed and mailed letters for business communications. Rock music was still controversial for many, having seized public attention only four years previously. The controversial movie of 1960 was Federico Fellini's *La Dolce Vita*. In that year John F. Kennedy (1917–1963) was elected president of the United States. Schools and public washrooms in much of the southeastern United States were still segregated, and lynchings were a vivid recent memory and still a latent threat. Aboriginal children in Canada were being forced to attend residential schools, where they were not allowed to speak their language or manifest their traditional culture. Although Inuit were not yet Canadian citizens, they had just formed the West Baffin Eskimo Cooperative— which remains the longest lasting artists' cooperative in Canadian history, one of the longest lasting in the world .

In previous chapters we analyzed why and how culture changes. This chapter applies the analysis and principles to some of the major aspects of contemporary cultural change. If we agree that "contemporary" artists are those alive and practicing today, we may focus on those same two "generations" over the fifty years from 1960 to 2010. Over that sweep of time there have been many cultural changes of great magnitude: advances in the levels of health and education, an overall reduction in starvation and poverty, the struggle between secularism and fundamentalism, the rise of a consumer society, the spread of feminism, the sexual revolution, and of course globalization, among others. Focusing on aesthetic culture, we undertake to encompass this complex period in relation to seven aspects of contemporary cultural change:

- Cultural Change Beyond Boundaries
- The Dominance of Cities
- Cultural Tourism
- The Knowledge Economy
- The Communications Revolution
- Human Rights and Identity
- Intracultural Change

CULTURAL CHANGE BEYOND BOUNDARIES

In the twenty-first century, aesthetic culture—the expression of meaning through the senses and through our imagination—is no longer contained within the limits of individual media, institutional types, or economic and national boundaries. To be sure, we still feel that the place where an artist lives or works is of significant interest, helping us understand "where the artist is coming from." And we still choose whether to go to a movie, a theater, or the art museum. But when the curtain goes up we are as likely to see dancers perform with cinema as with other dancers; in the concert hall we may see swirling colors pulsed by electronically generated sounds; and at the art museum, we may be confronted by something called an "installation" enveloping us in the scents of cinnamon and curry. And not a painting in sight.

Museums today are questioning the conventions of how they display works of art, archaeological artifacts, or specimens of nature. There was a time when science museums were organized by discipline: geology, paleontology, botany, and so on. Today, natural history museums are engaged with chemistry, genetics, and biology all at once as they seek to explain ecological and environmental issues. And they are as likely to invite an artist as a scientist to comment on an issue—or to create a work of art.

For more than a century, art museums classified their galleries by country, school, and style, such as "Dutch Landscape School" or "American Abstraction." For visitors who didn't understand these categories in advance, museums were difficult to navigate. Nor were visitors helped much by the tiny labels that stated only the title of the work, the artist's name, birth and death dates, country of birth, the name of the donor and a mysterious catalogue accession number. Just as soldiers were told to tell their enemies only their name, rank, and serial number if captured, so enemies learned to respect the integrity of the work of art, allowing it to speak directly to the visitor, by giving only these few scraps of information.

In the early 1990s, London's Tate Gallery (as it was then called), under the leadership of its then relatively new director (now Sir) Nicholas Serota, started a revolution—reinstalling the permanent collection along thematic lines and providing descriptive labels of about ninety words in length for each work of art. Previously, gallery themes—concepts or ideas around which works might be grouped together—were only for changing or temporary exhibitions, never for the permanent collection, the meaning of which was assumed to be "permanent." Now Tate curators began grouping their permanent collection around themes such as "the image of women in the twentieth century," grouping paintings and sculpture representing women and asking visitors what they thought the works implied about the changing role of women in the past hundred years.

Serota went a step further by deconstructing the notion of a "permanent collection display." He challenged Tate curators to reinstall the galleries once a year, calculating that by reselecting and reinstalling the collection each year the Tate could significantly boost the number of works on view over time from 20 percent of the collection, which was what could be shown at one time prior to the creation of Tate Modern. Gail had been asked by the Tate (now Tate Britain) to lead a visitor audit to determine what visitors thought about the gallery and about the changes. We used a broad range of research techniques such as tracking and observing visitors throughout the building, surveys, and personal interviews in the galleries, and we learned a lot of simple but important things:

- Visitors are hungry for more information about art.
- Visitors don't like getting lost.
- Visitors look for signage, and will use it when it's clear.
- Visitors really enjoy the thematic installations as long as they can find the title and explanatory panel.

One day, Gail overheard a loud argument among the curators and communication staff who were planning the next reinstallation of the collection. At issue was what to call the gallery of Victorian paintings: the traditional, much-favored title was "Victorian Painting 1870–90"; the communications staff preferred something more provocative, such as "Sex and Death in Victorian Painting" (since that was the subject matter of many of the canvases). Gail suggested that we print the two titles on cards, go down to the galleries and interview visitors to see which they would choose. After a few days of sampling, she reported back that visitors across all the demographic groups liked both approaches, but wanted them put together as one. So the gallery would be called "Sex and Death in Victorian Painting: 1870–90."

Today it seems obvious to mix timeline and themes—but just twenty years ago, that was a hard boundary to cross. Based on the success of the Tate, many galleries and museums began to cross these boundaries—and more. The idea that the museum has a single, anonymous voice of authority has been replaced in many museums with labels that attribute their words to different curators—a label has become a matter of interpretation, not of eternal truth. When the Art Gallery of Ontario (AGO) reopened in Toronto in 2009 after a major expansion, the curators, led by artist and curator of Canadian painting Gerald McMaster, dismantled the boundary between aboriginal artists and their contemporaries who happened to be non-aboriginal, white, mainly male, and professionals. Aboriginal art is now presented throughout the AGO galleries in dialogue with European-descended art—in many cases subverting assumptions about the art and culture of both.

Why is this borderless world the pervasive trend in culture today? We are reminded of the principle that *"each social group seeks its own values in the art it patronizes."* Today the vast majority of people who are successful in maintaining coherent social groups "for themselves," not just "in themselves," groups that have the need and desire to patronize aesthetic culture in some way, are successful to the degree that they are engaged with global exchange in all aspects of life and work—natural resources, information, finance, transportation, high-value-added products, or in knowledge sectors such as teaching and research. These new patron groups—whether sponsoring festivals, endowing museums, investing in films, buying art, or supporting university departments of cross-cultural studies—see their own values best realized in crossing boundaries. It is to be expected that there are pockets of patronage that prefer a more inward-looking and bordered approach—and these exist in every location to one degree or another. In chapter 8 we explained how the highly branded, borderless culture of the oil economy in Saudi Arabia is still severely constrained by the power of the Kingdom's religious leaders. Less obvious contrasts characterize patronage groups elsewhere, but the character of the contrast is almost everywhere the same—while some conservative patronage persists in maintaining a traditional focus on one medium, the new patronage arising from individuals, organizations, or institutions experiencing the cross-disciplinary world of today responds enthusiastically to the initiation of new content by artists intent on crossing boundaries.

The island republic of Singapore provides a fascinating example of how quickly cultural change can go from "inward-looking" to "beyond boundaries." Twenty years ago, when its main industry was the production of microchips for the world, Singapore was starting to create cultural infrastructure—museums and heritage preservation were for the first time "affordable" in this relatively new country, founded in 1965. In 1990, just as we were finishing our work with *Glasgow's Glasgow*, the centerpiece exhibition of Glasgow's year as European Capital of Culture, Barry encountered a Singaporean delegation in the corridors of Glasgow City Hall and helped them to find the office of the director of all the City of Culture events, whom they wanted to interview because they wanted to learn more about how

Glasgow had transformed itself, so that they could apply the lessons learned in Singapore. Soon we were working with the Singapore government on master plans for the first postcolonial museums, including an exciting new art museum, Singapore's brilliant Asian Civilizations Museum (crossing borders of Asia's many countries and cultures), and establishing a National Heritage Board to administer them.

Prior to 1990, Singapore had been tearing down its architectural heritage. All through that decade, there were severe social and ideological restrictions on art, theater, and film subjects (sex and gender issues were not to be discussed) and style (radical or countercultural forms like installation and conceptual art were strongly discouraged). A lone art school struggled to survive, as parents insisted that their children study science or business courses only. A countercultural artist-run center in a former power station was often under surveillance, performance art shows were summarily closed, and artists in a few cases were arrested for "offensive" presentations. Tourists visited Singapore for shopping, or as a rest stop between the more interesting destinations in Asia all around it.

As education levels rose and a very high percentage of Singaporean youth were university-educated—many of them abroad—Singapore became an exporter not just of microchips but also of talent and knowledge. Singapore has a relatively small population of a few million people, so a permanent brain drain was a definite possibility, and would have posed a serious problem. But at about this time the Singaporean economy was becoming more diversified: knowledge-intensive biotechnology industries were now in the forefront. As the world's biggest port city trading in this increasingly diversified economy, Singapore had to become more open.

Today, the cultural scene in Singapore is also more open—instead of being suppressed the artist-run centers are subsidized, the art school is flourishing, architectural heritage is being preserved, and Singapore hosts art fairs and biennials. Changes in Singapore's material culture have developed new interests among potential patrons of the arts, in both the public and the private sector. To be sure, the context is very Singaporean, with a Singaporean level of control and centralization—but the edge of cultural change is always subtle. Singapore now strives to stimulate and support creativity, so that those Singaporeans who are educated abroad have good reason to come back and stay. Visitors who come to shop or between other destinations stay to explore what the island has to offer. Gail has more recently been helping Singaporeans to plan a new museum on an art-science theme—crossing borders again—that will be part of a bright new waterfront cultural and tourism complex.

In the early 1990s, almost no major Western museums of modern and contemporary art had a significant collection from so-called developing countries. The modern and contemporary art of India, Africa, South Asia, West Asia, and even Latin America was considered to be "not important," so it could be kept inside the safe boundaries of specialized museums of anthropology or ethnography. Even Western museums of Asian art resisted collecting and displaying the contemporary art of China, Japan, Korea, or South Asia: their collections were based exclusively on the ancient and classical arts of those countries, and they did not hire curatorial expertise in the contemporary field, so they were unable to change the situation. The Peabody Essex Museum in Salem, Massachusetts, was one of the few exceptions, pioneering the collection of art from these regions.

One of the turning points in changing the attitude toward contemporary Asian art was *Alors, La Chine*, a multidisciplinary exhibition at the Centre Pompidou in Paris in 2003. Two years earlier, the Chinese government had for the first time sponsored the travel of an exhibition of contemporary Chinese art to a Western country, a show called *Living in Time*; but in Berlin, as Zhang Yu, then president of the China International Exhibition Agency, commented, "the German art museum decided only to rent some side halls to us since they were not quite sure about the quality of Chinese art and our ability to organize the show. But after the opening, the German side began to regret this when they found the exhibition was so influential and popular. It might be the Germans' regret that made the French so determined this time."

Having learned from the German experience, the Centre Pompidou gave its main temporary exhibition galleries over to this large exhibition, comprising works by fifty leading contemporary Chinese artists, supplemented by a French collection of visual culture from China's cultural revolution and three outstanding objects of ancient, traditional Chinese art to set the contemporary work in context. *Alors, La Chine* included film, photography, and contemporary visual arts and music, making for a powerful experience of cultural change. Today, major art museums in developed countries are in competition to collect art globally and to build relationships with artists in so-called developing countries. Chinese contemporary art is most sought after, but Korean, Indian, Iranian, and Arab art are all gaining greater attention too. This new patronage further encourages artists in these countries to work and think beyond their boundaries as well.

Fifty years ago we all paid close attention to the choices that each participating country made to show in its national pavilion in the Venice

Biennale. Established in 1895, the Biennale was (and remains) a decisive art world event, manifesting the direction of cultural change in the visual arts globally and within the countries that maintain exhibition pavilions there. Today a great many cities around the world host these large juried exhibitions called biennials, which have become an alternative way for artists who do not fit into the preferred categories to enter the art world and to gain attention from patrons. The 2009 Sharjah Biennial, for instance, featured little-known Arab, Iranian, and other West Asian artists. Biennials themselves offer patronage, sometimes inviting artists as individuals or in groups, subsidizing their participation, creating a place where countries, cities, and the private sector can support their participation, and providing a meeting place for artists, media, galleries, museum curators, and collectors.

Just as permanent collection installations have gone thematic, so have biennials. Since its beginnings, the Venice Biennale has followed the tradition of world expositions with national pavilions representing the visual art of each participating country, as selected by curators appointed by those countries. Although these pavilions continue to be important at Venice, in the past decade the focus has shifted somewhat beyond the boundaries of these national pavilions to the galleries in the Arsenale and elsewhere that are used for major thematic exhibitions organized by the Biennale itself, which appoints a distinguished curator each year to explore a theme.

One of the earliest of these large biennial exhibitions to adopt this thematic approach was *Documenta*, inaugurated in 1955 in the city of Kassel in Germany. Under Hitler, any form of abstract art or art by Jewish artists, communists, and other "undesirables" had been branded "degenerate," ridiculed, confiscated, sold to make money for the Reich, or destroyed. A decade after the end of World War II, *Documenta* began the campaign to put German art and artists back in the central position they had occupied prior to 1933, with this series of large exhibitions organized by a curator selected for each show to demonstrate a thesis or explore a theme through his or her selections of contemporary art. The impact was to catapult German artists, audiences, and patrons into the global world of free expression and contemporary art. Originally a number of West German artists, and since 1991 some East German artists as well, have been among the most widely recognized visual artists in the world.

Today there are over several hundred biennials, from Santa Fe to Havana, from Singapore to Senegal. International film festivals play a similar role in stimulating and sustaining global creativity in cinema. Cannes, in the south of

France, famously provides the equivalent to Venice, with the Toronto International Film Festival rated second, along with more specialized festivals like the Sundance Film Festival in Park City, Utah, where "independent" films are often introduced. But international film festivals are powerful patronage instruments of cultural change all around the world. In 2009, for example, in the Arab world alone, the thirty-third annual International Film Festival was showing in Cairo, the ninth annual festivals in both Beirut and Marrakech, the sixth annual in Dubai, and the third annual Middle East International Film Festival in Abu Dhabi, while two new festivals started—the Tribeca Film Festival in Doha, and Doxbox, a documentary film festival in Damascus. These festivals offer an important alternative of "art films" to the Hollywood and Bollywood movies shown in the commercial cinemas of the region. Combined with the added patronage of the relatively few "art film" cinemas, now working together throughout the region in the Network of Arab Arthouse Screens, and cinema clubs in each city, these international film festivals have inspired a whole generation of creative Arab filmmakers.

The worldwide boom in international film festivals, biennials, music festivals of all kinds, drama festivals, art fairs, and "fringe" festivals of unofficial events associated with the major art festivals such as the Edinburgh Festival, results from four main factors:

- *The intensity and rapidity of cultural change,* which requires a more flexible format than can be provided by large institutions that need to plan their content three to five years in advance. Biennials and festivals are more of the moment and can take greater risks than large permanent institutions. International film festivals can take risks on new films or films by independent producers that cannot get access to the distribution channels for the standard Hollywood and Bollywood fare.
- *The need to develop new audiences in postcolonial societies,* which formerly did not control their own cultural production or undervalued their own art due to the principle of cultural domination that we noted in chapter 7. In many cases these new audiences are in regions where working people did not formerly have access to time and money to participate in aesthetic culture, either as artists or as a public for it. In these situations there is a deep and lingering mistrust of institutions that were formerly exclusionary—even when they no longer are. The more nimble and open arts festival format provides a more welcoming environment for these so-called nontraditional audiences.

- *The availability of resources* for relatively cheap travel for contemporary artists and their works. Because of the informality of most biennial and festival venues, works of art can be installed or performed at a relatively low cost (often using student help and casual labor), compared to what established museums, concert halls, or art centers require.
- *The growth of cities* and the consequent competition among them to attract a knowledge-based workforce, cultural tourists, and inward investment. Hosting an international film festival, biennial, or music or drama festival is a proven means to attract international attention, to draw intellectuals and artists to the city, and to engage with local artists, media, and knowledge workers. Mahmoud Kaabour, for example, is an internationally known filmmaker (celebrated for his 2004 film *Being Osama*), who was born in Lebanon but moved to Dubai in 2005, attracted by the Dubai International Film Festival, which he supplements twice a year with his own "Mahmovies" public screenings, in addition to producing his own creative work.

The distinguished Nigerian-born curator Okwui Enwezor summed up the significance of biennials in his address to the 2007 Asian Art Museum Directors' Forum (itself a significant beyond-boundaries event) in Singapore as follows:

> What Biennials have done is to truly help us re-imagine the notion of centers and periphery. We have, today, no longer one knowledge or artistic centre. Rather what we have is a deeply dispersed but not fragmented field of cultural production. . . . I think if there is anything that Biennials have done, it is really to put to rest, at least for the moment, the very notion that the centre is where all activities and canon formation happen.[1]

THE DOMINANCE OF CITIES

In 1900, only 10 percent of the world population lived in cities. The world was still mainly an agrarian planet. In 2008, for the first time in world history, half of the world's people lived in cities. And the proportion of people living in cities will continue to grow for the foreseeable future. The growth of cities is both a result and a cause of economic growth in non-agrarian societies: trade, industry, and the knowledge economy all benefit from concentrations of people. The twenty fastest-growing cities in the world today are in China, and China is the world's fastest growing economy.

Cities are growing in numbers and population throughout Asia and the developing world—making cities of Europe and the United States seem small in comparison. The number of megacities—cities of more than 10 million inhabitants—has climbed from five in 1975 to fourteen in 1995 and is expected to reach twenty-six by 2015. In 1900, the ten biggest cities in the world were in North America or Western Europe; today, only two are—New York and Los Angeles.[2]

Cities have always been catalysts for cultural change, but the rapid growth in the number and size of cities has sparked a quantum leap in cultural change because there has been a fundamental worldwide shift in who has access to surplus. Cities produce an enormous share of the gross domestic product (GDP) of most countries, and while it is generally true that these cities receive less return from central governments than they contribute, the preponderance of surplus wealth lives in cities. As we noted in chapter 7, *culture changes with changes in access to surplus.* That is why we are seeing and will continue to see an increasing *urbanization* in the content of aesthetic culture. Urbanization refers not only to the focus on city life and living in close quarters, but also to the multicultural dimension of urban life. Most cities are places where people from many cultures speaking many languages live in close proximity. This is obviously true of cities in countries with high levels of immigration, like Toronto, which has been called the most multicultural city in the world because it has the highest number of populations of 20,000 or more each speaking their own language. But it is equally true of cities where one might not expect such diversity: Abu Dhabi, for example, the capital of a relatively small country, has people from two hundred different nationalities living in it. Abu Dhabi is striving to be more than an oil economy: to become a world financial and cultural center. Just two generations ago Abu Dhabi was a fishing village. The culture its leaders patronize is an intensely urban, cosmopolitan one: on Saadiyat Island, across a bridge from the city center, they are building the Guggenheim Abu Dhabi, designed by Frank Gehry of Los Angeles; the Louvre Abu Dhabi, designed by Paris architect Jean Nouvel; and the Sheikh Zayed National Museum, designed by Sir Norman Foster of London, the last of which will be operated with the assistance of the British Museum. A Maritime Museum, designed by the distinguished Japanese architect Tadao Ando, is slated for development a few years later. The Saadiyat Island Cultural District that will accommodate these major cultural institutions and others is based on highly sophisticated urban best-practice models.

The growth of cities increases the speed of cultural change exponentially because cities concentrate the four main motors of cultural change that facilitate patronage: artists, market mechanisms, education, and institutions that collect, display, and disseminate aesthetic culture.

1. *Art production*: a critical mass of artists live there, colocated with the technology needed to produce and reproduce their art, such as sound studios, rehearsal and recording facilities, publishers, and high-tech companies.
2. *Market mechanisms*: theaters, galleries, auction houses, publishers, impresarios, distributors, arts managers, arts funders, antique shops, booksellers, critics, and—essentially—patrons.
3. *Art education*: universities and colleges where artists can teach and produce more artists, as well as more of their own art due to the patronage of the educational institutions.
4. *Cultural institutions* that collect and display aesthetic culture—concert halls, museums, galleries, theaters, cinemas, festivals, archives, and libraries.

At one time these motors coexisted in just a few cities, such as Paris, London, and New York. Today, the least attractive city will have more such infrastructure than the most picturesque village. Auction houses have decided to move their sales to where the new markets are—so that major sales are now held in cities in emerging markets, not just in the traditional art capitals. As commercial galleries like Durand-Ruel transformed the art market of the nineteenth century in Paris with their solo exhibitions, so the global spread and increased activity of the auction houses are transforming the market today. Auctions not only take place in new locations around the world (Sotheby's in Doha, Christie's in Dubai), they also occur far more frequently. The *investment* value of art patronage has sharply increased, as works circulate back through the auction houses more frequently, with the most volatile prices—high or low—going to contemporary art. Art investment companies have emerged as forces of growing significance in this marketplace. Together with the increased importance of branding noted in the previous chapter, this heightened emphasis on investment is reflected in the content of the works for sale, which must be universally exchangeable as investments, whether they come from a Manhattan loft or a Mumbai slum.

Art fairs—which colocate commercial galleries from around the world in different cities for a few days of sales to the patrons of that city—are also providing local and regional access to the world's art markets. These art fairs also provide the opportunity for regional galleries to colocate with famous international galleries—thereby providing opportunities for artists to become known internationally and acquire more access to more patrons. Miami becomes a global art center once each year due to the success of its art fair, along with the warehouses in which local patrons show their collections of contemporary art. Like biennials, art fairs have gone global: in 2007 and 2008, Abu Dhabi imported selections from the Paris art fair, but by 2009 Art Abu Dhabi was able to go it alone as an art fair, attracting the participation of galleries eager to bring their artists' work to this emerging new market.

Cities draw their populations from regions both near and far, bringing together people of diverse backgrounds and skills to work in their factories, service industries, and professions. A diversity of people living in close proximity creates new forms of social organization, new models of behavior, new identities, and new ideas. All these new dimensions of daily changing urban life stimulate artists to produce new content. Cities create wealth, so more of the potential patronage groups based in cities have access to surplus—including various levels of government, trade unions, professional organizations, multicultural organizations, and many more—as well as individuals of great wealth. In the medieval city, aesthetic culture was supported by the church, the craft guilds, and wealthy patrons in various strata. In larger nineteenth-century cities, we see evidence of somewhat more distributed patronage—the so-called middle class, industrialists, large corporations, academies, universities, working men's associations, city- and state-funded museums, libraries, and theaters. At that time, industry was located near sources of raw materials, or adjacent to transportation hubs for those raw materials. The transformation of the Manchester Ship Canal from a filthy postindustrial transport hub to a sparkling cultural hub called Salford Quays around the Lowry, as we described in chapter 1, is symbolic of the transformation of cities to the knowledge-based economy—which has the capacity to attract artists and to generate support for artists, schools, and universities where they can teach, media companies that need their creative abilities, consumers who will buy the products they design for homes and offices, and institutional patrons—including the cities themselves.

Although biennials can be effective means to attract artists, patrons, and media attention to cities, biennials are temporary. Cities must compete not just to attract talent—entrepreneurs, scientists, scholars, inventors, and artists—but also to convince them to live and work on their streets permanently. In the sixteenth and seventeenth centuries, artists wanted to visit and if possible to live at least for a while in Rome, as did Nicolas Poussin (1594–1665) for most of his later life; academies in France and Prussia established annual competitions for artists with prizes consisting of a year's residence in Rome. In the eighteenth and nineteenth centuries, with Europe's patronage base shifting northward, the dream of most artists was to live and work in Paris. Eventually, in the twentieth century, London and New York provided the necessities of artistic life—cheap studios and places to live, galleries, theaters, concert halls, art consumers, and institutions to display the art and stage performances. In our own time even much smaller cities understand that they need to provide a supportive environment for the "creative class."

In the late 1980s, Glasgow, which had suffered severely from a precipitous decline in its traditional industries of steel and shipbuilding, opted to become "a city of culture." At the time, the idea was preposterous. Stimulated in part by the challenge to win the coveted designation of European Capital of Culture—which conferred a marketing brand as well as prestige—Glasgow developed a twenty-five-year plan to become a major cultural capital. The hard-working Scottish city won "Capital of Culture" status for 1990, and made its year with that title so successful that it established an international benchmark still referenced today for how culture can transform a city and produce measurable economic impact. As curator and assistant curator of *Glasgow's Glasgow*, the keystone exhibition of that year, Barry and Gail were thrilled to be part of the excitement. A few years later Barry wrote a supporting letter for a Canadian artist competing for a grant to study in Europe, and when the young artist won we were surprised—but we should not have been—to learn that he had chosen Glasgow as the city to live and work in with the grant.

Even before winning the Cultural Capital designation, Glasgow had embarked on a project to attract artists to live in the city, and to retain the best of the graduates of its outstanding art college in the building designed in the Art Nouveau style by its world-famous architect and designer Charles Rennie Macintosh (1868–1928). Why would artists want to live in Glasgow rather than London or Edinburgh? The answer was (and still is) cheap rent, plus flexible conditions, including zoning that allows live-work space, and an understanding landlord. To achieve the latter, the city supported the creation of a charitable organization to own, maintain, and manage artists' studios in the historic district called Merchant City. It worked. This became a model for cities and organizations all over the world—including a very successful group in Toronto called Artscape, an artist-run not-for-profit corporation that develops properties where artists can live and work. One of Artscape's projects is called the Art Barns because the group redeveloped as artists' spaces the streetcar barns formerly used to house and repair Toronto's streetcars. This visionary artist-led development also provides spaces for the local community, including greenhouses and a weekly farmers' market. In the Washington, DC, exurb of Alexandria, Virginia, artists' quarters have been provided in a former torpedo factory, while in Tallahassee former railway buildings were converted to artists' use.

These examples demonstrate the emergence of artists themselves as patrons. This is by no means new: one of Canada's greatest painters, Lawren Harris (1885–1970), well-endowed financially as a member of the Harris family, who were partners in the agricultural implement firm Massey Harris, himself became a patron of the national landscape school, the Group of Seven (discussed in chapter 7), when he commissioned construction of the Studio Building in which Tom Thomson (1877–1917) lived and painted his greatest canvases, based on the sketches he had made in the northland; Harris also chartered the railway car that took several members of the group on a historic trip into the Algoma country of midnorthern Ontario. Many of today's and tomorrow's artist patrons are not at all wealthy, but are being patrons in collaboration with each other and with powerful partners in the private and public sectors (especially city governments) who have access to financial and property resources. The artists bring their resources of time, expertise, and creativity, with the result that they are helping to reshape some twenty-first-century cities as centers of the knowledge economy.

The cooperative movement—in which producers work together in a democratic way to reduce costs and get better control of their markets—has long been strong in Italy, and as professors Larry and Judy Haiven of St. Mary's University in Halifax have shown, it includes artists' cooperatives. The Associazione Nuova Scena, for example, is a theatrical collective founded in Milan in 1968 (the year of the "*sessantotto*" generation of students' and workers' movements throughout Europe) by playwright, director, and composer Dario Fo and his actress wife Franca Rame. Having turned an abandoned factory into a collective, they also built movable stages and toured Italy with their cooperative company, Il Capannone di Via Colletta. In 1969 they produced Fo's *Mistero Buffo* (*Comic Mystery*), which presents contemporary satirical monologues in the *commedia dell'arte* tradition, sparking the widespread *teatro di narrazione* (narrative theater) movement, which recovers the story-telling roots of popular theater. Thus Fo's and Rame's collective united the role of creative artists initiating new content with that of a fruitful new source of patronage, encouraging other artists to go further in developing this kind of topical theater.

While Nuova Scena continues today in Bologna with repertory theater, traveling shows, and a theater school, Fo and Rame left it in 1970 due to political differences and founded still another cooperative, Collettivo Teatrale La Commune, which continued to produce improvisatory plays based on current events in Milan. In 1973, after the premiere of their play *Accidental Death of an Anarchist*, which identified the complicity of the Milanese police in the murder of a political radical, Fo was assaulted and imprisoned, while Rame was abducted, tortured, and raped by a neo-fascist group with ties to the *carabinieri*. Heroically, she returned to the stage two months later to resume her satirical monologues on the police. By the 1980s, Fo and Rame began to receive the national and international acclaim that was their due: in 1997 Fo was awarded the Nobel Prize for Literature, while Rame has been elected to the Italian Senate.

Although Italy is a major center of artists' collectives, they have been developed elsewhere. The small southern Ontario city of St. Catharines, which has long had an active artists' cooperative movement, is now home to the CRAMart Gallery, which boasts that it is Canada's *smallest* gallery, print-making facility, and studio complex. The collective's manifesto proclaims a confident local-global approach, opposing fast food along with "all other types of mediocrity." Small as it is, this artist-run center is hosting an international print exhibition in exchange with artists from Santiago, Cuba's second city. There is a political edge to CRAMart's "beyond borders" approach, because St. Catharines is near Niagara Falls and Canada's border with the United States, where the blockade of Cuba is still in effect.

One of the longest-lasting artists' cooperatives of major significance is the West Baffin Eskimo Cooperative, established by James Houston (1920–2005) and the Inuit artists in Cape Dorset in 1959 and still flourishing today with annual exhibitions and sales of the sculpture, prints, textiles, and drawings of the artist members. Houston, himself an artist later known for his own work in glass, as well as his writing, had discovered the power of Inuit carving originally in Arctic Quebec in 1948, and created a whole new patronage base by organizing exhibitions of these soapstone carvings first in major Canadian cities and then in New York. In 1950 he moved on to Cape Dorset on Baffin Island in the High Arctic, where he transformed the entire community into one of the most intensive art-producing places on the planet. Having recognized the communal pattern of life among the Inuit in the Arctic, Houston had little difficulty convincing the artists to form a cooperative that has been successful ever since in providing them with well-equipped studios to work in, while ensuring optimal returns to the artists themselves.

In 1959, with the new market for Inuit sculpture well established, Houston encouraged the Cape Dorset artists to begin print-making (initially by sealskin stencil, subsequently by almost all graphic techniques) and mounted their first exhibition in Stratford, Ontario, where patrons of Canada's Stratford Shakespearean Festival were delighted to discover it. In a prescient act of patronage, Houston personally commissioned the first drawing by Kenojuak Ashevak, thereby helping to start the career of one of the greatest of these artists; as shown in the 2009 film made about him after his death by his filmmaker son John Houston, unlike previous patrons from the south who had told the Inuit artists what they wanted them to draw, James Houston simply asked her and others to use their imagination and draw what came to mind.

Cape Dorset today is almost entirely dedicated to visual art, with a higher density of artists than Greenwich Village, as one New York visitor remarked. Larger cities often concentrate the artists in one area—Beijing, Mumbai, Bilbao, Los Angeles, Berlin, and many other cities today all have significant artists' districts. District 798 in Beijing—another example of artists serving as patrons—is astonishing for its size and diversity. The name

Kenojuak Ashevak, *The Enchanted Owl*, 1960, stonecut on laid paper, 61 x 66.1 cm (24 x 26 in.), printed by Eegyvudluk Pootoogook, National Gallery of Canada, Ottawa. Photo: Reproduced with permission of Dorset Fine Arts.

Scene from Yan Pei-Ming's 2009 exhibition *Landscape of Childhood* at the Ullens Center for Contemporary Art, District 798, Beijing, which opened in 2007. Photo: Liang Guo, courtesy of UCCA.

"798" references the district's original function as Electrical Factory 798, which was literally part of China's military-industrial complex. It is now a charming tree-lined urban district featuring reuse of its brick Bauhaus-style factory buildings as galleries, studios, shops, and cafes. After the success of his Long March Project, begun in 2002, of staging cultural events along the route of the Red Army's strategic Long March throughout China led by Mao Zedong in the 1930s, artist and curator Lu Jie founded the Long March Gallery here, one of the first major independent art galleries in Beijing, with exhibitions that attract major curators from all over the world. District 798 is so vital that it attracted a Swiss couple, Guy and Miriam Ullens, to establish a museum there with their collection of contemporary Chinese art in a former factory building with high ceilings and capacious galleries.

CULTURAL TOURISM

Tourism may be seen to have its origins in the pilgrimages that have long been features of many religions and are still today a major reason for international travel in many parts of the world. One world travel organization estimates that each year 350 million people travel within their own country or internationally for religious reasons alone. Today the pilgrimage destination that attracts the largest numbers of people is Mecca, which welcomes 3 million pilgrims annually during the *Hajj* and 10 million people throughout the rest of the year. One of the great tourist voyages historically was that of the Berber scholar Ibn Battuta (1304–1369), who set out from his native Tangier in Morocco in 1325 on a pilgrimage to Mecca and returned home after twenty-nine years of travel, having explored much of west and central Asia and north Africa in what would today be called cultural tourism. His journal is still considered one of the greatest works of travel literature.

Pilgrimage is motivated by religious faith, but pilgrimage also stimulates learning and cultural change. The *Canterbury Tales* of Geoffrey Chaucer (1345–1400), a contemporary of Ibn Battuta, reveal how Christian pilgrimage in the fourteenth century provided opportunities for people of different social backgrounds to interact in ways that would not have been possible in the otherwise strictly stratified world of monastery, castle, and guild.

The secularization of European society meant that travel in the early modern period became more of an enjoyable cultural experience, especially for the younger members of families who could afford to undertake it. Young English aristocrats especially enjoyed the "Grand Tour" of the ancient and more recent cultural attractions of Italy. By the eighteenth century, tourism was firmly situated as a broadening educational activity for those who had completed their formal education. Educated people were still a minority of the population, so educational tourism remained a minority activity— although one of great economic significance to the main tourism destinations. Artists were themselves great tourists, traveling to see renowned works of art in situ (especially important before the age of mechanical reproduction), and to experience the architecture and landscapes of Italy, Greece, or other countries. They recorded what they saw and learned, and often created new content from the mixing of cultures they experienced—*the intercultural principle* in action. E. M. Forster (1879–1970), himself a great traveler, explored this content most sensitively in relation to Italy in his 1908 novel *A Room with a View*, then again even more profoundly in his last great novel, *A Passage to India*, published in 1924. In his 1949 novel *The Sheltering Sky*, an American expatriate in Tangier, Paul Bowles (1910–1999), vividly evoked the distinction between tourists and another sort of travelers who don't intend to return. The outstanding films made of these novels stimulated a creative and critical awareness of cultural tourism still further.

In the last sixty years, international tourism has grown thanks to increasing levels of education, the economic capacity to generate greater surplus, the statutory requirements for paid vacations won by the struggles of trade unions, and the availability of cheap long-haul travel and relative peace (compared to the previous years characterized by two world wars). In 1950, there were 25 million international tourists; by 2005, the number had risen to an estimated 800 million.[3]

People travel for many different reasons—only about 50 percent is for leisure and recreation. The term *"cultural tourism"* has appeared in tourism research only during the period that we have been working in the field. Gail remembers asking an official in the Canadian government's Tourism Ministry how many people visited Canada for cultural purposes and being told that "there is no such thing as cultural tourism." He was right at the time, since even the term had not yet been defined. Gail proposed one of the earliest definitions in a study our firm did in 1993 on cultural tourism for the Government of Ontario: *"visits by persons from outside the host community motivated wholly or in part by interest in the historical, artistic, scientific, or lifestyle/heritage offerings of a community, region, group or institution."*[4]

This definition is still in use today by tourism organizations that identify scores of tourists' special interests (from sex and gambling to sports and the environment). It is estimated that about 15 to 20 percent of tourists travel specifically for the purpose of cultural participation. The percentage rises dramatically to 60 to 80 percent when cultural participation is considered to be *part* of the motivation for the trip.[5] The percentage varies with the destination country: by way of example, for Britain, which offers few swimmable beaches and little or no skiing, the percentage of tourists who are motivated in part by culture and heritage is an extremely high 85 percent. Since the data shows that people who are motivated by culture spend more money, stay longer, and do less damage to the environment (mainly because they have more advanced levels of education than the "mass tourist"), countries, cities, and regions have set about using some of their surplus to patronize cultural offerings and to present destinations that were formerly focused on the mass "sun and sea" tourists as places appealing as well or instead to those tourists wanting to experience heritage, the arts, theater, and local gastronomy (as opposed to beer and fast food). Only 5 percent of the revenue from "mass tourism" stays in the country that hosted it.[6] This low rate of return combined with the high environmental costs of mass tourism is causing many countries to reevaluate their tourism strategies and reorient toward cultural tourism.

For the past twenty-five years, Spain has been the world leader in this transformation—creating cultural destinations in every city and region of the country, which is not difficult given its rich heritage, but which nevertheless has required a major cultural shift and a huge investment. Spain is an especially interesting example of the interpenetration of social-political cultural change with aesthetic cultural change. During the fascist dictatorship of Generalissimo Francisco Franco (1892–1975), which lasted from the end of the Spanish Civil War in 1938 until after Franco's death, much of Spain's political and artistic culture was suppressed, especially the culture of Spain's vibrant regions. Many of Spain's leading artists had openly supported the Loyalist democratic cause, such as the great dramatist and poet Federico Garcia Lorca (1898–1936), who was executed by Franco's soldiers. Speaking the Basque, Galician, or Catalan languages publicly was forbidden, political protest was viciously repressed, and there was active censorship of all forms of art and media. The tiny neighboring principality of Andorra was the only place that Catalan writers could hope to publish during those years.[7]

Today, fewer than forty years after Franco's death in 1975, a social democratic government has instituted laws to protect women's and gay rights, has opened its door to immigration, and has developed a dynamic culture of film, media, architecture, and the visual arts. The regions and their cultures are flourishing under generous provisions of autonomy that satisfy all except the extremist Basque separatist movement, ETA. This cultural change has been so rapid that a generation for whom Picasso was demonized coexists with a young generation for whom anything goes.

In this context, it is not so surprising that in the Basque country—not far from the traditional Basque cultural center of Guernica, which was immortalized by Picasso in his memorial painting for its suffering after it had been bombed by Nazi planes supporting Franco—the business and civic leaders of the city of Bilbao and the province of Bizkaia decided in the 1980s that the city's long-term survival required a transition from an industrial economy to a postindustrial one—a reorientation comparable to the one taking place in Glasgow at about the same time. Approaching the Solomon R. Guggenheim Foundation in New York in 1991 with the idea of creating a branch museum of modern and contemporary art in Bilbao was one element of a complex plan including new road and transportation systems to transform the city. The Basque government mobilized US$125 million in public funds, Frank Gehry was appointed architect in 1992, and the project broke ground in 1993, opening on time and on budget in 1997 to international excitement and rave reviews. The economic benefits of the 800,000 to a million visitors the Museo Guggenheim Bilbao (MGB) receives annually are said to have repaid the initial investment many times. They have also sparked an urban transformation including new hotels, a concert hall and convention center, a new transport system, additional museums, and the much-needed renovation of the nearby Museo de Bellas Artes de Bilbao, which houses an outstanding collection, but did not previously have a building capable of preserving and presenting its holdings adequately. Today, the MGB anchors a river esplanade where the local community gathers to stroll amidst sculpture and cafes, while the Bizkaia government has asked Barry and our Spanish company, Lordcultura, to help them plan a new museum of Basque heritage and culture.

Perhaps the biggest Bilbao story is the least known—that the museum's staff and board leadership was not content to remain a tourist destination. Between 2005 and 2009, Gail and Maria Fernandez Sabau (director of Lordcultura) facilitated two strategic planning processes with the MGB. One issue that museum staff wanted to address was whether the museum was a "tourist attraction" or a "real museum." Through a process of external interviews, research, and deep discussion with staff and board, it became clear that the museum is in fact performing the core museum roles of collection, display, education, and research—but that the strong Guggenheim brand has impeded public awareness of the intellectual contributions being made right there in the Basque country. However, it also emerged that the MGB was not adequately addressing the needs of the future creative economy. Staff and board leadership worked on this issue, so that in its 2009–2012 strategic plan, the museum clearly articulates one of its four strategic goals as: *"To promote, support and develop artistic and educational projects that generate knowledge in the context of the Basque Country's creative economy."*

Among the museum's seven strategic initiatives for the year 2020 are two that address this goal:

- to create an expansion of the MGB in nearby Urdaibai to combine art with nature, and a location for collaboration and innovation; and
- to establish specialized training programs for museum professionals in collaboration with local universities.

Santiago de Compestela in Galicia in northern Spain was and still is one of the great Christian pilgrimage sites, from the medieval period to today. Pilgrims still follow the symbol of the shell (an early example of branding) along the pilgrimage trails that extend from Germany and the Low

Countries through France and across the breadth of Spain. The city of Santiago de Compestela has a huge cathedral, where mass is performed for pilgrims who arrive at the destination throughout the year. In 1999, New York architect Peter Eisenman and his firm won the competition to design the new "City of Culture" on Mount Gaies in Santiago, intended to "echo" the existing pilgrimage city. We were privileged to play a small role in helping to plan the City of Culture, which consists of around 50,000 square meters (c. 500,000 sq ft) of cultural buildings, including a library, archive, exhibition center, the Galician National Museum, and a performing arts center. The first phase of the complex is scheduled to open in 2012. Its current challenge is to animate the magnificent buildings designed by Eisenman with compelling content.

Galicia is not alone in linking cultural tourism to religious pilgrimage. In Saudi Arabia the holy city of Mecca is considering the development of several cultural projects, including a library and cultural center to promote global dialogue. Saudi Arabia's other holy city of Medina also has plans to add cultural destinations of broad educational value for both its large resident and pilgrimage populations.

Patronage provided by tourists and the tourism industry can be a spark for cultural development. However, sustained cultural change requires commitment to excellence, creativity, and the development of human potential from within society itself—this requires patronage from the public sector. Ultimately, as our work at Bilbao demonstrates, the success of cultural tourism depends on the involvement of the creative resident population.

THE KNOWLEDGE ECONOMY

There has been a fundamental shift in the world economy as more and more industrial and consumer products are produced far from the countries of the North Atlantic—in China, India, Southeast Asia, and Latin America. The main economic growth in the so-called developed countries is in the financial sectors, technology, science, health, and culture—broadly referred to as the "knowledge economy." These are "clean, green jobs" that require comparatively higher levels of education. The work involves responsive thinking, complex communication, and nonroutine manual tasks. About 30 to 40 percent of the workforce in advanced economies is considered to be part of the "knowledge economy."

In this circumstance, attracting and retaining an educated and highly literate workforce is key to the economic success of a city, a region, or a country. Recent research indicates that literacy is a more accurate predictor of economic growth than the more commonly used measure of the number of years spent in school. A 1 percent rise in literacy scores (relative to the international average) is associated with a 2.5 percent rise in labor productivity and a 1 percent rise in per capita GDP.[8]

Acquisition of literacy depends not only on the effectiveness of formal education, but also on a social context that encourages literacy—a society that provides material and immaterial incentives for parents to read to their children and to encourage children and young people to ask questions and seek answers on their own and communities that provide libraries and access to museums, theaters and cinemas, and the ideas, works of art, and human expression to be found in them. In the early 1960s, the revolutionary Cuban government proved that it is possible to transform the literacy levels of an entire country by mobilizing all readers, young and old, to teach the illiterate; within one year, this literacy campaign, having inspired thousands of all ages to teach many more thousands in every city, town, and farm, had achieved nearly complete basic literacy in Cuba. In this regard it is of the greatest concern that publishers in all the Arab countries together currently translate into Arabic for the widespread population from Morocco to Iraq fewer books than Greek publishers translate into Demotic Greek, a language spoken only by the much smaller population of that one country and the Greek diaspora around the world. For Arabic speakers and readers to participate in global cultural change, they must gain greater access to the scholarship and literature of the rest of the world.

Literacy is not only acquired by children and young people—it is a lifetime learning process for adults. University of Toronto economist Richard Florida and his colleagues have explained that all people are creative: about 30 percent of the workforce is employed in jobs that are creative, but the creativity of the other 70 percent is largely wasted. He has demonstrated that an environment that attracts and retains creative people is also one that stimulates all of its residents to be creative. Florida identifies this environment as the "three Ts" of economic development: technology, talent, and tolerance. Of these, tolerance and openness to diversity of people and of new ideas is most difficult to achieve—especially in societies where a single religion is in a position of authority and control.

Our second principle in chapter 7, that *the quantity of surplus controlled by a social group impacts the extent of its culture*, is demonstrated by the ways in which aesthetic culture flourishes in communities where the knowledge economy is strong and where city government, banks, and technology companies control enough surplus to invest in the patronage of arts festivals. *Nuit Blanche*, for example, is a one-night sunset-to-sunrise arts festival that features installations and performance events in public spaces and cultural institutions, turning a whole city center into an open air art center. All existing cultural institutions and cultural industry venues can participate, but there are also installations and performances in otherwise unoccupied public or borrowed spaces all over the city. The first such event was initiated by the mayor of Paris in 2002, and has since been taken up by various cities, including Toronto since 2005. Paris claimed the participation of 1.5 million people at 150 venues in 2008, while Toronto counted almost 800,000 people in the streets with an immediate economic impact of Cdn$13.5 million in the same year. For Paris, Toronto, Lima, Rome, Tel Aviv, Sao Paulo, and the 200 other cities presenting an annual *Nuit Blanche*, the benefit of harmonious participation in aesthetic culture is much more significant than any direct economic impact—because such a festival fosters the creation of an open, tolerant, and creative cultural context for residents and visitors, a context that is needed to nourish and sustain the knowledge economy.

HUMAN RIGHTS AND IDENTITY

In the aftermath of the devastation of World War II—and specifically due to the revelations of the Holocaust in which millions were murdered because they were Jewish, or Gypsies or communists or gay—a new concept of human rights was born. This concept of the inalienable and indivisible rights of every human being on earth is expressed in the *Universal Declaration of Human Rights* (*UDHR*), which was adopted by the United Nations in 1948. Although *The Rights of Man*, written in 1791 by Thomas Paine (1737–1809), fused ideas from the American Revolution with those of the French Revolution, intending them to be of universal application, in practice the rights conveyed by the republican constitutions of either country could be enjoyed only within that country and to a greater or lesser extent in its dependencies—which Napoleon invoked almost immediately as a justification for conquest.

Thus while there had been efforts throughout human history to declare, codify, and safeguard human rights within one country or for one group, the *Universal Declaration* was the first time that most nations agreed on a concept of human rights that applies to all human beings irrespective of their nationality, citizenship, gender, race, religion, or ability, and made the enforcement of human rights the subject of multilateral action by the nations of the world. The *Declaration* is the most universally accessible document in human history, having been published in more than three hundred languages. In order to make it effective, after two decades of extensive rewriting and negotiation, the text of the consequent *Universal Covenant on Civil and Political Rights* was adopted in 1976 by thirty-five nations, and became international law. The *Universal Declaration of Human Rights* and the subsequent international conventions and courts of law—although unevenly applied throughout the world—position human rights beyond boundaries and establish the idea of our common humanity in a robust and effective way.

A year before the 1948 *Declaration*, India became independent, and Pakistan was created. Within the next twenty years, most of the world's remaining colonies won their independence. Within twenty-five years of the *Declaration*, a powerful worldwide women's movement had forever changed the position of women in many parts of the world and continues to have a dynamic impact today. In South Africa, a little more than forty years after the *Declaration*, apartheid was finally defeated. Thus the concept of human rights has profoundly affected the social-political culture of our time.

Human rights law and practice is a part of social-political culture that is vital to our understanding of contemporary cultural change because the evolving appreciation of our common humanity has been the single biggest force to break through the cycle of race-, class-, and gender-based devaluation of other cultures. Human rights consciousness places a major brake on the operation of the principle of cultural domination that we outlined in chapter 7. It is worth noting that Article 27 of the *Universal Declaration of Human Rights* specifically applies to culture, stating that everyone has the right to freely "participate in the cultural life of the community." In the 1990s, the United Nations undertook wide-ranging research on cultural issues, including how indigenous cultures, cultural minorities and their languages, and in particular the "immaterial culture" of these peoples are threatened by powerful states and by pervasive technologies and commercialization. In 2001, the United Nations Educational, Scientific and Cultural Organization (UNESCO) unanimously adopted the *Universal Declaration on Cultural Diversity*, which explicitly stated the positive value of cultural diversity that had been implicit in the *UDHR*.[9] At the core of the UNESCO document is the statement that: *"as a source of exchange, innovation and creativity, cultural diversity is as necessary for humankind as biodiversity is for nature."*

Aesthetic culture has been participating directly in this flowering of human rights and diverse cultural identities. Without the *Universal Declaration of Human Rights* and subsequent international research and debate on the cultural implications of our common humanity, it is highly doubtful that we would be enjoying world music today. The sixth principle discussed in chapter 7 concerning valuation and devaluation of culture by powerful patrons, imperial powers, and dominant media continues be a major factor in how and why culture changes, but it is less powerful than it was prior to the 1948 *Declaration*, and loses power daily because in the realm of aesthetic culture, tremendous value is placed in our time on "identity"—the identity of the artists who create aesthetic culture and the identity of the audiences who participate in it. In the aftermath of the *Universal Declaration of Human Rights* we experience aesthetic culture as a dance of identities—sometime synchronous, sometimes in conflict—in an ever-changing dynamic.

In chapter 8 we noted the function of design in proclaiming group identity for peoples who work together in a common pursuit, such as the Indian peoples of Rajasthan and Gujarat who can be identified by the printed patterns on their cotton garments. We also observed that identity can be the content of works of art related to the values associated with the cooperative labor of a group. Now we can see that identity as the content of works of art is also rooted in our consciousness of human rights. Artists both within and outside a group may sense a need to affirm the identity of the group as a way of confirming respect for the rights of the members of the group. Similarly, patrons both within and outside the group may respond to that content in works of art if they are themselves aware of the group's identity, especially if it is or has been demeaned or disregarded.

Identity cards constitute the expression of identity in social-political culture. In periods of repression of certain groups, identity cards become critically important, and during the Holocaust the Nazis made the public expression of Jewish identity mandatory by requiring all Jews to wear a yellow Star of David. The great German Jewish artist Felix Nussbaum (1904–1944) evoked the anxiety centered on these social-political statements of identity with his powerful self-portrait glancing anxiously at us as he shows us his identity card in his left hand and turns up the collar of his coat to reveal the yellow star with his right hand. At the time, in the early 1940s, Nussbaum was living in hiding in Belgium, courageously walking to his secret studio each day where he had to paint, because the man who was sheltering him and his wife in a secret attic was afraid that German soldiers would smell the oil paint when they became suspicious and searched his home. The painting anticipates Nussbaum being stopped on the street—cornered, with the walls converging behind him—whereas in fact he and his wife were arrested in their hiding place, betrayed by a secret Gestapo agent, and sent to their deaths on the last train to Auschwitz late in 1944.

Painted in hiding in Brussels: Felix Nussbaum (1904–1944), *Self-Portrait with Jewish Identity Card*, 1943, Oil on canvas, 56 x 49 cm (22 x 19⅜ in.), Felix-Nussbaum-Haus, Collection of the Sparkassenstiftung, Osnabrück, Germany. Photo: akg-images. © Felix Nussbaum Estate/SODRAC (2009).

Painting based on the identity cards used in the Cultural Revolution: Zhang Xiaogang, *Bloodline Comrade No. 3*, 1996, oil on canvas, 130 x 100 cm (51³⁄₁₆ in. x 39³⁄₈ in.). Photo: Courtesy of the artist and PaceWildenstein, New York. © 2009 Zhang Xiaogang.

Identity cards were also required during the Cultural Revolution in China. In the 1990s, artist Zhang Xiaogang in his *Comrades, Bloodline,* and *Great Family* series of portraits based on these tiny images tellingly recalls how the sitters strove for neutral expressions, fearful that either a self-satisfied or a critical demeanor might suggest a counterrevolutionary disposition. Each portrait bears stains, yellow or darkening red-purple, as if something had fallen on the photograph. And each is invaded by thin red bloodlines, reminding us that the sitter might be implicated by his or her family connections with relatives suspected or convicted of counterrevolutionary tendencies. In an even more evocative series in the early years of this century, Zhang went further with a group of paintings called *Remember and Forget,* in which he allows his subjects for the first time to hint at expressing emotion. But after the fall of the Gang of Four and the end of the Cultural Revolution in 1976, it had become possible to reflect on this period thoughtfully, as Zhang's powerful paintings do: by the mid-1990s, his canvases were already representing China at the biennials in Sao Paulo and Venice. Having received enthusiastic patronage abroad, they are only now beginning to enter museum collections.

The impact of these paintings, from Felix Nussbaum to Zhang Xiaogang, shows the importance we attach to expressions of identity in our time. But both group and individual identity have also provided more positive content to much aesthetic culture, especially as they have been affected by the communications revolution. Manuel Castells, in his 1997 book *The Power of Identity,*[10] the second volume of his monumental work entitled *The Information Age: Economy, Society and Culture,* connects the rise of identity as an issue in social movements and political life to two contradictory impacts of information technology:

- people's reaction against global networks of capital flows, information, and power over which they (and their governments in many cases) have no control; and
- the increased capacity this technology provides for people to network.

The Internet augments our capacity to create networks both of individuals and of groups. Castells observes that there is a simultaneous growth in both individualism and communalism. One individual has many identities, both ascribed and actual, such as a historically rooted ethnic identity, a gender identity, a professional identity, a value-based identity (environmentalist or religious, for example), a leisure-based identity (gaming, music, or bridge), and thousands of other preferences. Web 2.0 and its social networking media capacities make it even easier for people to find others with common values and to build identity-based communities over time and space.

Hence there are more social groups than ever before, so our very first principle of cultural change—*all social groups have a culture*—helps us understand the sheer diversity of theater, music, and visual art that exists today. All social groups want to strengthen their positions in the world, gain more adherents, achieve social and political objectives, and attain a stronger economic base. Aesthetic culture is a powerful force for communicating values that are the basis of social cohesion, without which social groups die. The third principle—*each social group seeks its own values in the art it patronizes*—means that identity is necessarily going to be an important part of all aspects of today's culture.

Identity—both ascribed and actual—is based on shared values. These shared values influence the leading edge of patrons (those who are most attentive to economic and social change) and the initiating creative artists described in chapter 6 who are professionally attentive to social change. Perhaps this explains why surveys show that trust in social-political culture—government, corporations, the law, and journalism—is at an all-time low, whereas trust in aesthetic cultural institutions—especially museums and libraries—is at an all-time high. Patronage at all levels, poor to wealthy, responds to content rooted in creative artists' sense of their own identity—as a visit to an international film festival will attest.

One country where identity has been gloriously affirmed in a human rights context is South Africa, following the end of apartheid. Anthropological exhibits in the National Museum of South Africa in Capetown had to be reconsidered in the light of this major social-political change. We were directly involved in the planning and management of a new institution called Constitution Hill in Johannesburg, a permanent exhibition on the struggle and the ultimate victory of the antiapartheid forces—in Pudovkin's terms (see chapter 7), expressing the "pathetic grandeur" (both the pathos and the grandeur) of the African majority and their supporters.

Constitution Hill is located in the former Johannesburg prison where at different times both Mahatma Ghandi and Nelson Mandela were held prisoner, and is adjacent to the new Constitutional Court, which is linked to and partially constructed from bricks taken from the former jail. The new South African Constitution conveys full language and cultural rights on no fewer than eleven constitutive nations of South Africa, so its Constitutional Court was built to respond to the challenge of reconciling cultural with individual human rights—addressing, for instance, the conflict between a culture that severely limits women's rights and the human rights of individual women within that culture. The exhibition that Lord Cultural Resources helped to plan and then managed for the first two years of its operation evokes not only the suffering within the walls of the prison, but also aims to identify the fundamental human rights issues and points to the ultimate victory of the Africans. Constitution Hill opened on South Africa's National Human Rights Day, March 21, 2004. At the opening ceremony, Thabo Mbeki, then president of South Africa, hailed it as "the transition of a negative colonial space to a positive, creative one."

The establishment in Canada of a new national museum, the Canadian Museum for Human Rights (CMHR), is another significant case study of the twin impact of identity and human rights culture. The dream of the late Canadian philanthropist Israel Asper (1932–2003), the CMHR is scheduled to open in Winnipeg in 2013 in a landmark building designed by the Pritzker Prize–winning American architect Antoine Predock, with exhibitions to be designed by the New York exhibition designers Ralph Appelbaum Associates. The mission of the new museum is to explore and enhance the public's understanding of human rights and to encourage respect for others—hence the name of the museum is not "of" but "for" human rights.

"9 Films for Projection by William Kentridge," 2004, Constitution Hill, Johannesburg, South Africa. Event organized by Artlogic. Photo: John Hodgkiss. Image courtesy of Artlogic.

Gail has been involved in planning the museum from its earliest days, helping to develop the concept originally with founder Israel Asper and subsequently with the board that is continuing to develop the original idea. Throughout 2009 she and Lord Cultural Resources' consultants and researchers assisted the museum's staff to gather human rights stories from across Canada. In meetings with linguistic groups (because in Canada, language is a human right), with indigenous peoples, disabilities groups, African Canadians, labor, immigrants, women, homosexuals and transgendered persons, victims of sexual or institutional abuse, prisoners, ethnic groups, human rights advocates, artists, and many others, it is apparent that people who experience human rights violations in their current situation, or have experienced such violations in the past or in community memory, feel themselves to be somehow diminished, sometimes expressed as "less human" because of the violation. What is so very moving is the power and potential of the hope people hold that their experience and their identity will be validated through representation in this museum. This aspiration is particularly significant when we realize that many of those who have experienced human rights abuses are among those who have considered themselves excluded from cultural institutions, or have in reality been effectively excluded from them—for reasons of education, time, money, or lack of self-confidence. Yet these very people place great hope in the transformative power of a museum dedicated to human rights.

As societies around the world strive to become more inclusive, museums and other cultural institutions will increasingly become places of conscience. There are seventeen museums of conscience that constitute the International Network of Sites and Museums of Conscience in ten countries. They include historic sites and museums associated with the Holocaust, the Museum of Tolerance in Los Angeles, Constitution Hill, the House of Slaves on the island of Goree in Senegal, and sites like the National Underground Railroad Freedom Center in Cincinnati. Many more museums of conscience already exist that are not members of this network, and more are being founded as the culture of human rights continues to grow and transform aesthetic culture.

THE COMMUNICATIONS REVOLUTION

In 1966, Barry became editor of Canada's national art magazine, then entitled *Canadian Art*. Publisher and graphic designer Paul Arthur, later known for inventing the terms "signage" and "wayfinding," had audited a course on the communications revolution taught at the University of Toronto by philosopher Marshall McLuhan, and wanted to change the magazine to com-municate what he had learned about how the world was changing. In 1967, publisher and editor together deconstructed the magazine, renamed *artscanada*, printing each article to maximize visual impact in its own format—some bound like traditional magazine articles, others opening in accordion folds to offer a photo spread, still others unfolding to provide subscribers with a full-color poster. Reviews and current art news were covered in an eight-page or sixteen-page tabloid newspaper, and a sound recording—in those days still a 45 rpm record—was included with each issue, along with an attractive cen-ter spread. All the disparate parts were gathered together, to the despair of librarians, in what instantly became known as "the mag in a bag."

The communications revolution has come a long way since then. When we started Lord Cultural Resources in 1981, we still wrote our first reports on a typewriter, using white-out tapes to correct each page to get a fair copy that could be reproduced. Our travels were trailed by piles of paper trans-mitted to hotel business offices by the fax machine, trying to keep us abreast of developments back in the office. Clients read drafts on paper and expected to wait weeks for any corrections they requested. The speed and ease of dig-ital communications has transformed how we do business, but it has also changed everyone's expectations of what is possible, resulting in incessant demands for speed-up in communications and for maintaining contact with everyone else. Networking makes new forms of social groups—and there-fore new kinds of patronage—possible.

Today, newspapers are threatened by news sources on the Internet, with a significant number ceasing publication. Publishers of fiction and poetry are similarly challenged by e-books. The music industry, already transformed repeatedly throughout the twentieth century by advances in recording tech-nology, is in the process of being revolutionized, as it becomes possible for musicians and composers to bring their work directly to the attention of mil-lions of listeners and viewers via the "social networks," thereby circumventing the need for contracts with the recording companies, which have scrambled to catch up. The practice of architecture and design has been transformed as the drawing table has been replaced by the computer workstation, where three-dimensional modeling of a proposed building or product can be con-ceived and instantly transmitted to a client or colleagues around the world. Even more traditional art forms like painting and sculpture have been affected by the universal availability of images, as entire collections of major museums can be posted online. Long-standing patterns of patronage of the cultural industries are being fundamentally disrupted and replaced by new ones.

This massive change in both material and social-political culture has led to widespread cultural change, demonstrating the quantitative principle expressed in chapter 7. More art is being produced and distributed to more people than ever before, creating cultural change in sheer numbers. Media corporations no longer control the distribution of music, which is now available on the Internet. Film is becoming more and more freed from the control of studios and production companies. The speed-up in cultural production will lead to more and more rapid cultural change—the quantitative principle in action.

One of the attractive features of technological change is the capacity for social networking and personal engagement. Participating in cultural activities on the Internet and other media such as television that can be linked to the Internet provides opportunities for everyone to evaluate the experience, register their vote (and see it tabulated instantly), contribute comments and ideas, and forward all this to friends and acquaintances. Is this engagement a form of cultural participation, or is it a form of consumption? The pop-up advertisements that accompany most of the visual culture on the Internet immediately suggest a consumerist approach, by which is meant a closed rather than open-ended engagement. Like any other consumer good, the Internet moment is ingested and used up once your response is recorded.

Does the new communication technology provide an extension of civil society—an extension to our creative capacities—or is it a new form of mass entertainment that provides the illusion of participation? In the spirit of Theodor Adorno's phrase quoted earlier in this book, "entertainment is betrayal," some highly conscious Internet users are campaigning to build on the potential of social networking on the Internet to ensure that it keeps its creative potential for global participation in aesthetic culture. In the coming years we can expect to see a huge expansion of participatory Internet-based culture as the patronage for it expands and the revenue streams become more stable. We can also expect research to help us understand whether this form of participation is an extension of human creative capacity or a seductive deception—or possibly both.

INTRACULTURAL CHANGE

Some 150 million people—2.5 percent of the world's population—live outside their country of birth. This is not in itself a large number, but the cultural impact over the generations and the centuries is enormous.

There are many reasons for migration, such as traumatic dispersal of people through war, conquest, and genocide; search for food and work; pursuit of trade; furthering colonial ambitions; and the desire to reunify families. Indeed, migration—whether voluntary or forced (and it is sometimes almost impossible to distinguish between these)—is fundamental to human development.

One result of this migration process is the creation of diasporas—identity groups strongly attached to a distant homeland. Another result is the mixing of cultures among diasporic peoples, with each other and with those who have been settled in the region for longer. From DNA research we know that our differences are not "racial" or even physiological; our differences are cultural. As intermarriage and other forms of ethnic and racial mixing occur among people, new hybrid cultural forms emerge. This process of mixing is not new. What is new is the growing acceptance of *metissage* as an accepted part of life. Historically people of mixed ethnicity were marginalized or ostracized, and their language and culture were usually invalidated by the "originating" cultures. Whether it is the Metis in Canada (a mixture of indigenous people and French immigrants), the Nyonya of Malaysia (a mixture of Chinese and Malay people), the Creoles of the Caribbean and Latin America, or any others of the hundreds of mixtures to be found around the world, all have had to struggle for political rights and recognition of their language and their culture.

Multiculturalism is a strategy used to support the survival of diasporic cultures. As noted in chapter 7, this policy was initiated and enacted by Canada starting in the 1960s to encourage respect for immigrant communities and the forms of cultural expression they brought from their homelands. Patronage for multiculturalism, which has subsequently been instituted in many other countries, comes principally from government and from the diasporic communities themselves.

Interculturalism, also noted in chapter 7, refers to the more recent interest in collaboration and dialogue between and among different cultural groups. It is an important improvement on multiculturalism, since it encourages interaction among multiple cultures, resisting the tendency for each ethnic identity to live in its own world, cut off from the others and from the mainstream society they are in.

In the future, as there is an increased recognition of the rights of people to their identity, there will be a greater focus on intraculturalism, by which is meant experiencing the dialogue of cultures from the inside, from the perspective of plural identities. Playwright, actor, and director Wajdi

Mouwad, the associate director of the outstanding 2009 Avignon Festival in France, perhaps best exemplifies this plural identity: born in Lebanon in 1968 and forced to emigrate to France as a child because of the civil war there, he was denied French citizenship papers when still a teenager. He emigrated to Québec where he studied at the National Theatre School in Montreal, and went on with a brilliant intracultural career, creating the first Québécois-French theater company, leading Francophone theater at the National Art Centre in Ottawa, writing plays and directing theaters on both sides of the Atlantic. The pluralism of his cultural experience—Lebanese, French, Québécois, Canadian—invests in his work a profound understanding of the human condition. One of his current projects is a collaboration with the renowned historian Natalie Zemon Davis on a theatrical version of *Trickster Travels*, her biography of al-Hasan al-Wazzan (also known as Leo Africanus, c. 1486/8–c. 1532), the sixteenth-century geographer who lived a rich intracultural existence in the Muslim, Jewish, and Christian worlds of Spain, Africa, and Italy.[11] Dr. Davis, author of *The Return of Martin Guerre*, which was already the subject of a popular film, specializes in discovering, analyzing, and recounting stories of men and women who cross boundaries of gender, geography, and identity to connect in a divided world.

This is the intracultural principle to which we alluded in chapter 7 that will form the basis for aesthetic culture in the twenty-first century. Creative artists of today who are responding to this principle will be finding their way to patrons who are experiencing interculturalism as an essential part of their lives. Cultural change is likely to generate many more novels, films, and all other forms of art, architecture, and design rooted in this intracultural reality.

PARTICIPATING IN CULTURAL CHANGE

Cultural change continues as we write, and as you read. We are all participating in it, whether we like it or not! For that reason we have established a website, www.culturalchange.ca. We invite you to visit it, contribute your comments to it, and participate in the ongoing story of cultural change.

Your contributions need not be limited in scope to the arts alone. We have focused this book on the principles of change in aesthetic culture, but it is clear in every chapter that aesthetic cultural change is deeply entwined with changes in material, physical, and social-political culture as well. So we invite everyone to participate in the website and to provide your insights on the theory and practice of cultural change.

Notes

1. Okwui Enwezor, Asian Art Museum Director's Forum 2007, Singapore Art Museum, 2007.

2. Charles Landry, *The Art of City Making* (London: Earthscan Publications, 2007), 22–23; Fareed Zakaria, *The Post-American World* (New York: W. W. Norton, 2008), 90.

3. Landry, *The Art of City Making*, 169.

4. Lord Cultural Resources in association with the Economic Planning Group of Canada and Eck Talent Associates, *Strategic Directions for Ontario's Cultural Tourism Product*, March 1993.

5. Lord Cultural Resources and Brain Trust Communications, *Ontario Cultural and Heritage Tourism Product Research Paper*, February 2009.

6. Landry, *The Art of City Making*, 175.

7. Barry and our Spanish firm Lordcultura have worked with the Andorran Ministry of Culture on plans for a National Museum where Andorra's historic role as a center for peace and democracy may be celebrated.

8. Richard Florida, *The Flight of the Creative Class* (New York: HarperBusiness, 2005), 33–34.

9. The United Nations Educational, Scientific, and Cultural Organization, Paris, November 2, 2001. The *Universal Declaration on Cultural Diversity* was unanimously adopted by all member nations.

10. Manual Castells, *The Power of Identity* (London: Blackwell, 1997).

11. Natalie Zemon Davis, *Trickster Travels* (New York: Hill and Wang, 2006).

Further Reading

A BIBLIOGRAPHY of all the works of literature or books about all the cultures and works of art discussed in this book would be vast. We restrict this comparatively brief bibliography to a selection of books of criticism or interpretation of culture, mostly in English. Many are referred to in the text, but all may lead to further understanding of cultural change.

Adorno, Theodor W. *The Culture Industry: Selected Essays on Mass Culture.* Edited by J. M. Bernstein. London: Routledge, 1991.

Adorno, Theodor W., and Max Horkheimer. *Dialektik der Aufklarung: Philosophische Fragmente.* 2nd ed. Frankfort am Main: Fischer Verlag, 1969 (1st ed., 1947).

Arnold, Matthew. *Culture and Anarchy.* Cambridge: Cambridge University Press, 1957 (1st ed., 1869).

Arthus-Bertrand, Yann. *Earth from Above.* Translated by David Baker. Revised and expanded ed. New York: Harry N. Abrams Inc., 2002 (1st ed., 1999).

Auerbach, Erich. *Mimesis: The Representation of Reality in Western Literature.* Translated by Willard R. Trask. Princeton, NJ: Princeton University Press, 2003 (1st ed., 1946).

Bell, Clive. *Art.* London: G. P. Putnam's Sons and Chatto & Windus Ltd., 1914.

Benhabib, Seyla. *The Claims of Culture: Equality and Diversity in the Global Era.* Princeton, NJ: Princeton University Press, 2002.

Blackaby, James R. *Revised Nomenclature for Museum Cataloging: A Revised and Expanded Version of Robert G. Chenhall's System for Classifying Man-Made Objects.* Lanham, MD: AltaMira Press, 1995.

Bourdieu, Pierre. *Distinction: A Social Critique of the Judgement of Taste.* Cambridge, MA: Harvard University Press, 1984.

———. *The Field of Cultural Production: Essays on Art and Literature.* Edited by Randal Johnson. Cambridge: Polity Press, 1993.

———. *The Rules of Art: Genesis and Structure of the Literary Field.* Cambridge: Polity Press, 1996.

Bourdieu, Pierre, and Alain Darbel. *The Love of Art: European Art Museums and Their Public.* Translated by Caroline Beattie and Nick Merriman. Cambridge: Polity Press, 1991.

Braudel, Fernand. *Civilization and Capitalism, 15th–18th Century.* 3 vols. Berkeley: University of California Press, 1992.

Burtynsky, Edward. *Oil,* with essays by Michael Mitchell, William E. Rees, and Paul Roth. Gottingen, Germany: Steidl Publishers, 2009.

Carson, Rachel. *Silent Spring.* New York: Houghton Mifflin, 1962.

Castells, Manuel. *The Information Age: Economy, Society and Culture.* Vol. 2, *The Power of Identity.* Malden, MA, and Oxford: Blackwell Publishers, 1997.

Centre Pompidou. *Elles @ Centrepompidou: Artistes femmes dans la collection du Musee National d'Art Moderne, Centre de Creation Industrielle.* Paris: Centre Pompidou, 2009.

Cohen, Robin. *Global Diasporas: An Introduction.* Seattle: University of Washington Press, 1997.

Davis, Natalie Zemon. *Trickster Travels: A Sixteenth-Century Muslim between Worlds.* New York: Hill and Wang, 2006.

Deleuze, Gilles, and Felix Guattari. *What Is Philosophy?* Translated by H. Tomlinson and G. Burchill. London: Verso, 1994.

Economic Development and Cultural Change. Chicago: University of Chicago Press, Journals Division, 1952–.

Edwards, David. *Artscience: Creativity in the Post-Google Generation.* Cambridge, MA: Harvard University Press, 2008.

Engels, Friedrich. *The Condition of the Working Class in England in 1844.* Moscow: Foreign Languages Publishing House, 1962.

Fernández-Armesto, Felipe. *Civilizations: Culture, Ambition and the Transformation of Nature.* New York: Free Press, Simon and Schuster, 2001.

Florida, Richard. *The Flight of the Creative Class: The New Global Competition for Talent.* New York: HarperCollins, 2005.

———. *The Rise of the Creative Class—and How It Is Transforming Leisure, Community and Everyday Life.* New York: Basic Books, 2002.

Foucault, Michel. *Archaeology of Knowledge.* Translated by A. M. Sheridan Smith from the 1969 French edition. London: Routledge, 2002.

———. *The Order of Things: An Archaeology of the Human Sciences.* New York: Vintage Books, 1973.

Guilbault, Serge. *How New York Stole the Idea of Modern Art: Abstract Expressionism, Freedom and the Cold War.* Translated by Arthur Goldhammer. Chicago: University of Chicago Press, 1983.

Harrison, Lawrence E., and Samuel P. Huntington, eds. *Culture Matters: How Values Shape Human Progress.* New York: Basic Books, 2000.

Iyer, Pico. *The Global Soul: Jet Lag, Shopping Malls and the Search for Home*. New York: Vintage Books, 2000.

Klein, Naomi. *No Logo: Taking Aim at the Brand Bullies*. London: Flamingo, 2000.

Kroeber, A. L., and Clyde Kluckhohn. *Culture: A Critical Review of Concepts and Definitions*. Textbook Publishers, 2003 (1st ed., Cambridge, MA: Peabody Museum, Harvard University, 1952).

Landry, Charles. *The Art of City Making*. London and Sterling, VA: Earthscan, 2006.

Levi-Strauss, Claude. *Elementary Structures of Kinship*. Boston: Beacon Press, 1969.

Lewis-Williams, David. *Inside the Neolithic Mind: Consciousness, Cosmos and the Realm of the Gods*. London: Thames & Hudson, 2005.

———. *The Mind in the Cave: Consciousness and the Origins of Art*. London: Thames & Hudson, 2004.

Lord, Barry. *The History of Painting in Canada: Toward a People's Art*. Toronto: NC Press, 1974.

———, ed. *The Manual of Museum Learning*. Lanham, MD: AltaMira Press, 2007.

———. *Young Contemporaries '93*. London, Ontario: London Regional Art Gallery and Museum, 1993.

Lord, Barry, and Gail Dexter Lord, eds. *The Manual of Museum Exhibitions*. Lanham, MD: AltaMira Press, 2002.

———. *Planning Our Museums*. Ottawa: National Museums of Canada, 1983.

Lord, Gail Dexter, and Barry Lord. *The Manual of Museum Management*. 1st ed. London: HMSO Books, 1997; 2nd ed. Lanham, MD: AltaMira Press, 2009.

———, eds. *The Manual of Museum Planning*. 1st ed. London: HMSO Books, 1991; 2nd ed. Lanham, MD: AltaMira Press, 2001.

Lord, Gail Dexter, Barry Lord, and John Stewart Nicks. *The Cost of Collecting*. London: HMSO Books, 1989.

Lord, Gail Dexter, and Kate Markert. *The Manual of Strategic Planning for Museums*. Lanham, MD: AltaMira Press, 2007.

McLuhan, Marshall. *Understanding Media: The Extensions of Man*. London: Routledge Classics, 2001 (1st ed., 1964).

Murdock, George Peter, et al. *Outline of Cultural Materials*. New York: Taplinger Publishing, 1961 (1st ed., 1937).

Myerson, Jeremy. *Making the Lowry*. Salford: Lowry Press, 2000.

Narayan, Uma. *Dislocating Cultures: Identities, Traditions and Third World Feminism*. New York: Routledge, 1997.

Nochlin, Linda. "Why There Aren't Any Great Women Artists." *Art News*, vol. 69, January 1971.

Nussbaum, Martha, and Jonathan Glover, eds., *Women, Culture and Development: On Human Capabilities*. Oxford: Clarendon Press, 1995.

Pamuk, Orhan. *My Name Is Red*. Translated by Erdag M. Goknar. New York: Vintage Books, 2001.

Pirenne, Henri. *Medieval Cities: Their Origins and the Revival of Trade.* Princeton, NJ: Princeton University Press, 1969 (1st ed., 1927).

Rectanus, Mark W. *Culture Incorporated: Museums, Artists and Corporate Sponsorships.* Minneapolis: University of Minnesota Press, 2002.

Ridley, Matt. *Nature via Nurture: Genes, Experience and What Makes Us Human.* New York: HarperCollins, 2003.

Said, Edward. *Orientalism: Western Conceptions of the Orient.* Harmondsworth, UK: Penguin, 1991 (1st ed., 1978).

Scruton, Roger. *Beauty.* New York: Oxford University Press, 2009.

Singapore Art Museum. *Asian Art Museum Directors' Forum 2007.* Singapore Art Museum, 2007.

Singerman, Howard. *Art Subjects: Making Artists in the American University.* Berkeley: University of California Press, 1999.

Stallabrass, Julian. *Art Incorporated: The Story of Contemporary Art.* Oxford: Oxford University Press, 2004.

———. *Internet Art: The Online Clash between Culture and Commerce.* London: Tate Publishing, 2003.

Tawney, R. H. *Religion and the Rise of Capitalism: A Historical Study.* New introduction by Adam B. Seligman. Edison, NJ: Transaction Publishers, 1998 (1st ed., 1926).

Throsby, David. *Economics and Culture.* Cambridge: Cambridge University Press, 2001.

Tolstoy, Leo. *What Is Art? and Essays on Art.* Oxford: Oxford University Press, 1930.

Wallinger, Mark, and Mary Warnock, eds. *Art for All? Their Policies and Our Culture.* London: Peer, 2000.

Weber, Max. *The Protestant Ethic and the Spirit of Capitalism.* London: George Allen & Unwin, 1930.

Williams, Raymond. *Culture and Society: 1780–1950.* London: Chatto & Windus, 1958.

———. *Keywords: A Vocabulary of Culture and Society.* London: Fontana Press, 1976.

Zakaria, Fareed. *The Post-American World.* New York and London: W. W. Norton & Co., 2008.

Index

About the Authors

BARRY LORD and **GAIL DEXTER LORD** are best known as copresidents of Lord Cultural Resources, the world's largest firm specialized in the planning and management of cultural institutions and programs. Celebrating its thirtieth anniversary in 2011, the company has completed over 1,700 cultural planning and management assignments in more than 45 countries around the world. About fifty cultural planning and management professionals provide their services from offices in Toronto, New York, Paris, and Madrid, along with project offices wherever they are needed—currently in Bahrain and Saudi Arabia. With the objective of "creating cultural capital," the company's services include management consultancy of all kinds, exhibition development, facility planning, and recruitment and training programs, always for cultural institutions. Their clients have included the Louvre, Tate, Museo Guggenheim Bilbao, the Art Institute of Chicago, the Los Angeles County Museum of Art, and many more.

Gail and Barry are almost as well known as coauthors of a textbook that has been used in museum studies programs around the world, *The Manual of Museum Management* (2nd ed., 2009), which has been translated into Chinese, Georgian, Russian, and Spanish. They are also coeditors of *The Manual of Museum Planning* (2nd ed., 1999) and *The Manual of Museum Exhibitions* (2003), both of which are the favorites of architects and designers. In 2007 Barry edited *The Manual of Museum Learning*, while Gail coauthored *The Manual of Strategic Planning for Museums* with Kate Markert. All of these manuals are published by AltaMira Press.

Gail was born in Toronto, and graduated with a degree in history from the University of Toronto, where she organized a famous Pop Art Festival.

By that time she was already an art critic for Canada's largest-circulation newspaper, the Toronto *Star*. She went on to teach photography and film students at Ryerson University and edited several books, eventually coediting the world's first book on museum planning—*Planning Our Museums* (1983)—with Barry. As a museum planner she has played a leading role in the development of many new museums, including The Lowry in Salford, England, the Museum of the African Diaspora in San Francisco, and the Canadian Museum for Human Rights in Winnipeg.

Barry was born in Hamilton (forty miles west of Toronto) and graduated with a degree in philosophy from McMaster University there before pursuing graduate studies in the history and philosophy of religion at Harvard. He began his cultural work as an actor, apprenticing at Canada's Stratford Shakespearean Festival, and as a publishing poet, while completing the National Gallery of Canada's postgraduate museum training program. He was editor of Canada's national art magazine, *artscanada*, and author of the well-known *History of Painting in Canada*. Having served as a curator of art, director, and chief of education services at several Canadian museums, Barry developed a methodology for museum planning while directing capital funding programs for the National Museums of Canada. He has been actively involved in the planning of many museums around the world, including the Frist Center for the Visual Arts in Nashville, the Singapore Art Museum, and the Hong Kong Heritage Museum.

Gail and Barry continue to work together with their colleagues on the development of cultural facilities worldwide, currently including the King Abdulaziz Center for Knowledge and Culture (iTHRA) in Saudi Arabia, the West Kowloon Cultural District in Hong Kong, and Longwood Gardens in Pennsylvania. All of their projects and all of their life experiences have involved them with artists, patrons, and the public, and have provided exhilarating experiences of cultural change.